THE
NUMISMATIST'S TOPSIDE
COMPANION

VOLUME EIGHT
EDITED BY Q. DAVID BOWERS

PUBLISHED BY BOWERS AND MERENA GALLERIES, INC.

ISBN 0-943161-54-1

Published by:
Bowers and Merena Galleries, Inc.
Box 1224, Wolfeboro, NH 03894

All rights concerning this book are reserved by the copyright owner. Written permission is required for the reproduction of any information in this book, except for brief excerpts used in a review in a newspaper or magazine.

The cover art is by Jennifer Rose of Wolfeboro, New Hampshire.

© 1994 by Bowers and Merena Galleries, Inc.

Table Of Contents

Introduction
By Q. David Bowers ..... page 5
A Coin By Any Other Name
By Q. David Bowers, from The Numismatist, 1993 9
B. Max Mehl: The 1913 Nickel Man
By Thomas S. LaMarre, from Rare Coin Review No. 64, Spring 1987 17
A New Grading System
By Fred Schwan, from Rare Coin Review No. 64, Spring 1987 21
The Mint's Balancing Act
By Thomas S. LaMarre, from Rare Coin Review No. 66, Autumn 1987 27
The Coin Market is Alive and Well
By Dr. Joel J. Orosz, from Rare Coin Review No. 83, Spring 1991 33
A Book From 1889
By Q. David Bowers, from "The Joys of Collecting," Coin World, 1993 43
This and That
From Rare Coin Review Nos. 85 & 86, Autumn 1991 and Spring 1992 45
The 1964-D Peace Dollar
By Q. David Bowers, from "The Joys of Collecting," Coin World, 1993 49
The "Thrill of the Chase" with Carson City Mint Coins
By Weimar W. White, from Rare Coin Review No. 71, Winter 1988 51
Lyman H. Low Tells His Story
By Lyman H. Low, from Kingswood Galleries' Barrington Sale, August 1990 57
Supergrade Coins
By Scott A. Travers, from Rare Coin Review No. 90, Winter 1992 65
To Err is Human (and Can be Funny)
By Q. David Bowers, from "The Joys of Collecting," Coin World, 1993 71
Two (Numismatic) Resolutions for a Happy New Year
By Q. David Bowers, from "The Joys of Collecting," Coin World, 1993 73
Researching the 1894-S Dime
By James G. (Jim) Johnson, N.L.G., from Rare Coin Review No. 64, Spring 1987 75
Question and Answer Forum
From Rare Coin Review Nos. 86 & 87, Spring and Summer 1992 83

The Numismatist's Topside Companion

Trade Dollars
By Q. David Bowers, from "The Joys of Collecting," Coin World, 1993 87
A Fabricated NE Sixpence
By Andrew W. Pollock III, from Rare Coin Review No. 80, Autumn 1990 89
Let's Hear it for the Collector
By Q. David Bowers, from Rare Coin Review No. 93, September/October 1993 93
Hard Times Tokens
By Q. David Bowers, from "The Joys of Collecting," Coin World, 1993 97
Thomas L. Elder
By Thomas S. LaMarre, from Rare Coin Review No. 70, Autumn 1988 99
New Exhibit Ideas
By Q. David Bowers, from "Coins and Collectors," The Numismatist, 1992 105
Aspects of Collecting
By Hugh Cooper, from Rare Coin Review No. 76, Spring 1990 109
Buy, Beg, or Borrow These Two Books
By Col. Bill Murray, from Coin World, 1992 113
Minor Coinage of the 1870s
By R.W. Julian, from Rare Coin Review No. 77, Early Summer 1990 117
Getting Started
By Q. David Bowers, from "The Joys of Collecting," Coin World, 1993 123
What is Important?
By Q. David Bowers, from "The Joys of Collecting," Coin World, 1993 125
Join the Club
By Q. David Bowers, from "The Joys of Collecting," Coin World, 1993 127
This and That
From Rare Coin Review Nos. 86 & 87, Spring and Summer 1992 129
6,000 Year-Old-Advice
By Weimar W. White, from Rare Coin Review No. 79, Summer 1990 133
Improvements at the Bureau of Engraving and Printing
By Day Allen Willey, from Rare Coin Review No. 71, Winter 1988 137
Experiments with Aluminum Coins
By Thomas S. LaMarre, from Rare Coin Review No. 86, Spring 1992 139
Coin Market Cycles
By Q. David Bowers, from "Coins and Collectors," The Numismatist, 1993 145
Action at the Local Level
By Q. David Bowers, from "The Joys of Collecting," Coin World, 1993 151
The Copper Company of Upper Canada
By John J. Ford, Jr., from Rare Coin Review No. 65, Summer 1987 153
Did You Know?
From Rare Coin Review No. 92, March/April 1993 165
Reminiscences of Julius Guttag by His Son
By Alvin Guttag, from Rare Coin Review No. 66, Autumn 1987 169
The North West Company Token
By Thomas S. LaMarre, from Rare Coin Review No. 69, Summer 1988 175
The 1804 and 1823 "Restrike" Cents
By Q. David Bowers, from "The Joys of Collecting," Coin World, 1993 181
Machin's Mills Bicentennial
By Gary A. Trudgen, from Rare Coin Review No. 64, Spring 1987 183
Call to Arms—Collectors Unite!
By Q. David Bowers, from "The Joys of Collecting," Coin World, 1993 189

Introduction

by Q. David Bowers

Welcome to *The Numismatist's Topside Companion*. For those who live in the middle of the Mohave Desert or on top of Pikes Peak, "topside" is a nautical term referring to the upper side of a sailing vessel, particularly a sporting sailboat. The name is derived from a suggestion by our own Ray Merena, who was invited to come up with a title for one of the four issues of the current "Companion" series. Come to think of it, Ray's boat is of the motorized variety, so I guess that topside can refer to one of those, too.

The purpose of the "Companion" books is just that—hopefully, the present volume will be a nice go-along on trip, a weekend, or an adventure—who knows, possibly even on a boat.

Between these two covers you will find contributions from many "name" writers in our hobby, among whom are Thomas S. LaMarre, Fred Schwan, Dr. Joel Orosz, Weimar White, Scott A. Travers, James G. Johnson, Andrew W. Pollock, III, Hugh Cooper, Col. Bill Murray, R.W. Julian, Day Allen Willey, John J. Ford, Jr., Alvin Guttag, Gary A. Trudgen, and me.

I almost forgot to mention Lyman H. Low (his article begins on page 57). It isn't that this distinguished rare coin dealer is a reader of our publications, for he passed away many decades ago. This, as are a few other inclusions, is a reprint from an old periodical. In his day, Low was one of the best known dealers, and in the present era is especially remembered for his interest in Hard Times Tokens.

As these words are being written, I have just returned from a con-

The Numismatist's Topside Companion

vention of the Florida United Numismatists group in Orlando. In addition to participating in the lively auction which we conducted (the Lexington Sale), I had a chance to spend the best part of several days at the Bowers and Merena exhibit on the bourse floor. If there is one sentiment that was expressed more than any other, it was that people *really enjoy* reading about and learning about the history of coins. This to me seems somewhat paradoxical, in as much information in print deals with market prices, investment, and the like. However, perhaps I and my customers and visitors are prejudice, but as a group we all enjoy the story behind the coin.

With that in mind, many pages in *The Topside Companion* now await perusal.
—Q. David Bowers
March 1, 1994

A Coin By Any Other Name

by Q. David Bowers   1993

Written for The Numismatist, *the following is one of my favorites among all of the columns I have ever written for that magazine.*

"What's in a name? That which we call a rose, By any other name would smell as sweet," Shakespeare said in *Romeo and Juliet.*

"A definition is that which so describes its object as to distinguish it from all others; it is no definition of any one thing if its terms are applicable to any one other," wrote Edgar Allan Poe in *The Rationale of Verse.*

This article will probably please no one completely. The subject is numismatic nomenclature, an area with few rules but many ideas. The topic came up when *Numismatist* Editor Barbara Gregory and I were discussing the term *Liberty Seated,* as I prefer it. An article I had submitted for publication had come back with the phrase changed to *Seated Liberty.* I remonstrated that, for example, the *Guide Book* prefers *Liberty Seated,* and we also have the *Liberty Seated* Collectors Club.

Barbara countered by saying that in her opinion a noun should always come first, and an adjective second. Thus, *Seated Liberty.* If it were otherwise, then to be consistent with my preference of *Liberty Seated,* we should have, for example, 1856 *Eagle Flying* cent. I suppose we could also have the 1877 *Head Indian* cent.

After touching upon a few other terms, we both remembered that the Mint in its official news releases calls Lincoln cents "pennies," which is one of the first things the coin collector learns not to do. However, Dr. William H. Sheldon retitled his 1949 book, *Early American Cents,* as *Penny Whimsy* when it was updated and revised in 1958. Technically, a penny is a denomination of England and certain other countries, not of the United States. *Cent* is the official term used on this side of the Atlantic. However, does a cent become a penny if we call it one? Perhaps yes, perhaps no. Few would argue that if you call a cow a horse, it is still a cow. Thus, we are back to square one.

Before changing away from the cow-horse-cow analogy completely, I cannot help but mention that the ANA Mid-Winter Convention had its name changed a few years to the Early Spring Convention, even though it is still held in the winter, according to the calendar (but perhaps the calendar is wrong; never take anything for granted).

Let me also mention that we are dealing with flaws in the English language. *Operative* means *functioning,* whereas *inoperative* means *not functioning.* However, *inflammable* and *flammable* both mean the same thing, whereas one would logically think that inflammable would mean not subject to combustion. Then there is the subject of rhyming—thank goodness this article does not deal with numismatic poetry—and such English words as bough, through, tough, though, and so on. Pity the poor foreigner wanting to learn how to speak as we do!

Sometimes in numismatics a difference of opinion arises as to whether a word should be shortened for modern usage, such as *catalog* and *catalogue.* I have always preferred the latter, for when I was a kid one of my most consulted references was the *Standard Catalogue of United States Coins,* by Wayte Raymond. However, a couple years ago Carling Gresham wrote a commentary in which he felt that adding the "ue" was a bit stuffy and pretentious.

Should it be *luster* or *lustre*—I prefer the latter, which inclines toward the British usage. Is it *mint mark* (two words) or *mintmark?* Years ago, as in Augustus G. Heaton's treatise, *Mint Marks,* was usually two words. Today I see it often as one.

Grading nomenclature often displays variables. The official ANA designation is *Extremely Fine,* but often one sees *Extra Fine.* To my mind, extra means *superfluous,* not *very.* I note that PCGS on its holders has the abbreviation XF, which doesn't seem to be right either; EF is proper. Is it *About* Uncirculated, or *Almost* Uncirculated? I have seen both used. *About* takes preference.

I believe we can thank Ken Bressett for much of the nomenclature

A Coin by Any Other Name

we now use with regard to coin design types, especially among earlier issues in which there was little standardization. As editor of the *Guide Book,* and a close associate of that volume for many years when Dick Yeoman was editor, Ken created such terms as *Matron Head* for the 1816 cent, *Capped Bust* for the 1807 half dollar, and *Petite Head* for certain late-date large cents, among other terminology. (If someone else invented some of these terms, let me know and I'll put a note of correction in a future article.)

However, many of the terms that Ken didn't invent, but which have come to us by tradition, are not correct in a technical sense. For example, what nearly everyone calls the *buffalo* nickel should really be the *bison* nickel, for a bison is the quadruped depicted. Even better, it should be called an *Indian* nickel, for an Indian motif is on the obverse. Usually we call a coin by its obverse design, not the reverse (where the four-legged animal is), otherwise we would have the Monticello nickel instead of the Jefferson nickel, and the Great Seal half dollar instead of the Kennedy half dollar, etc.

One of the most erroneous popular terms is the *Mercury* dime. Depicted on the dime is Miss Liberty, a woman, with wings on her *head.* Mercury, the messenger of mythology, was a *male* and had wings on his *feet.* However, to say *Winged Liberty Head* dime is too complicated, and to simply say *Liberty Head* is to confuse it with, say, the 1892 Barber dime.

Speaking of coins of William Barber, perhaps these should be called Liberty Head dimes, quarters, half dollars, after the obverse motif. It is somewhat unusual, although not unprecedented, to name a coin after its engraver—but we do have the Saint-Gaudens double eagle and the Morgan silver dollar, among others However, we do not have the Fraser nickel (James Earle Fraser designed the Buffalo nickel—or is it the Indian Head nickel—or is it the Bison nickel?), the Flanagan quarter (Washington quarter), or Roberts half dollar (Kennedy half dollar).

The 1836 Liberty Seated (or Seated Liberty)—things are getting complicated)—silver dollar is popularly called a *Gobrecht* dollar, but an 1837 half dime or dime with precisely the same obverse motif is not known by the Gobrecht name.

About the time I was mulling over these things, Beth Deisher, editor of *Coin World,* telephoned, and in the course of our conversation I mentioned that I had just talked to Barbara Gregory, and was pondering ideas for an article on nomenclature. This caused Beth to mention that terminology was a problem at *Coin World,* too, and although a style guide had been printed for use of staff members, there were still many areas of disagreement. In particular, she brought up the Mercury dime situation. The next day a copy of the *Coin World* style guide arrived by overnight express. Among other things, I learned that for *Coin World* authors there are the following preferences:

Buyer's *fee* is preferred over buyer's *premium* or *juice.* I have heard the latter, particularly among younger dealers. Before then, I thought it had something to do with squeezing oranges. Now, some think it applies to squeezing bidders.

Standing room only: To quote *Coin World:* "When used as an adjective, hyphenate: 'The standing-room-only crowd filled the room to capacity.' When used as a noun, do not hyphenate: 'The bourse is filled to standing room only.' A standing-room-only crowd is one which every seat is filled and additional persons are forced to stand." I threw this in because in today's coin market, at numismatic seminars, and at conventions, it would warm all of our hearts to see some of these standing-room-only (I hope hyphens were supposed to be used here) crowd!

Canadian denominations: "There are no nickel, dime, quarter dollar, or half dollar coins among Canadian denominations. The proper usage is five-cent coin, 10-cent coin, 25-cent coin, 50-cent coin." I remember learning this the hard way when giving a talk before a group of Canadian numismatists. I was not more than a few minutes into my monologue when I noticed a persistently raised hand. I stopped, asked what the matter was, and was forthwith told that there was no such animal as an 1858 Canadian dime.

Coins without names: An interesting paragraph in the *Coin World* style guide informs users of the following: "Several U.S. coins have no commonly used name: Two-cent coins, silver three-cent coins, $3 gold coins."

Actually, the government referred to the silver three-cent piece as the *trime,* and I occasionally use it in some of my firm's auction catalogues (or *catalogs*), but it never has caught on. Next time one of my readers gets wrought up about grading terminology, surcharges on commemorative coins, certification services, or any other of the burning issues of the era, perhaps some of this energy could be diverted to making up a pet name for the two-cent piece or $3 gold coin. Both denominations are nice to collect, both are scarce, and perhaps they are deserving of better terminology. How about *twosies* and *threesies?*

Coronet: "Use Coronet instead of Liberty Head for the $1, $2.50, $5, $10 and $20 coins of the 19th century and early 20th century," the *Coin World* style sheets advise. Turning to the *Guide Book of United States Coins,* which was in existence before *Coin World* was even thought of (the first edition came out in 1946, whereas the first *Coin World* issue saw the light of day in 1960), I see therein that the gold dollar is referred to as the Liberty Head type, the quarter eagle is called the Coronet type, the half eagle is called the Coronet type, the eagle is called the Coronet type, and the double eagle (which has essentially the same design as the 1849-1854 gold dollar) isn't called anything—there is no title depicting the type.

Standing Liberty: the same *Coin World* reference tells me that instead of referring to certain 1917 quarters as Type I or Type II, if I were sitting in a desk at Amos Press out in Sidney, Ohio, working on the next issue of *Coin World,* I had better use the somewhat naughty-sounding "1917 Standing Liberty, Bare Breast quarter dollar," and the rather military "1917 Standing Liberty, Mailed Bust quarter dollar." I don't think I'll use these terms any time soon.

Stella: The same reference suggests that Stella always be capitalized, and at Bowers and Merena Galleries we usually do this as well. However, it doesn't make any more sense to capitalize Stella than it would to capitalize Dime, or Trime (we tried capitalizing these other two words here to see what they would look like). Similarly, *Coin World* suggests that trade in Trade dollars be capitalized but only if they are United States Trade dollars, not British trade dollars, or Canadian trade dollars. Personally, I never capitalize trade dollar unless it begins a sentence, such as "Trade dollars are the favorite coins of noted numismatic authority Bruce Amspacher."

Now, I move on to other ideas.

I like to capitalize coin grades, to avoid confusion. Thus, a Good 1804 large cent or a Fine example, doesn't refer to one of these scarce cents (or *pennies?*) that is *nice* or *desirable.* Instead, Good and Fine, if capitalized, have specific grade meanings. In numismatic literature, capitalization is often inconsistent. I also prefer to capitalize Proof, Mint State, and Uncirculated.

We all know our right hand from our left hand, but when you look at a Kennedy half dollar, which is the right wing of the eagle and which is the left? Procedure has never been standardized in this area, either.

On the *left* side of the coin is actually the eagle's *right* wing. To clarify this, sometimes writers say something convoluted such as "eagle's right (observer's left) wing," a phrase which I also have used. However, as the observer doesn't have a wing, it would probably be better to say something even more awkward: "Eagle's right wing (which the observer will see on the left side of the coin)." I think I will leave eagle wings behind now.

In the course of writing my book, *Silver Dollars and Trade Dollars of the United States: A Complete Encyclopedia*, I was urged by Eric P. Newman and several others not to refer to 1804 silver dollars as "originals" and "restrikes." Instead, the best term, apparently, is *novodel*, a word which I have employed. Usually (there are exceptions), *novodel* refers to a coin made for collectors or other purposes at a later date, by an official mint, of a specimen or variety of which no original (coin made in the year indicated) ever existed. Somehow, I think of *novodel* is a nicer word than *antedated fantasy* (which Eric P. Newman and Kenneth E. Bressett used in their book, *The Fantastic 1804 Dollar*) or Don Taxay's term, *piece de caprice*. To me, *restrike* is completely inappropriate, as this applies the issuance at a later date of coins from the *same dies* earlier to make originals in the year indicated on the dies.

Going further with the *restrike* term, it is believed that the 1851 Centered Date Liberty Seated (Seated Liberty?) dollar was either made from an obverse die cut in 1851 but never used then, or, more likely, a new die made at the mint a number of years later. If the die was never used to make original 1851 dollars, then we should not call these pieces 1851 restrikes today—but we all do.

Then there is the situation concerning government officials. When preceding a name I capitalize a title, such as Director of the Mint Donna Pope. However, after the name I do not, and it would be Donna Pope, director of the Mint. I capitalize Mint as it is a particular institution. Mint reports and other government documents are not at all consistent in this regard. Sometimes Director of the Mint, Secretary of the Treasury, and other terms are capitalized when all by themselves, and other times they are not. Speaking of Mint reports, did you know that what we call the Carson City Mint was almost never called this originally? It was referred to as the Carson Mint, or the mint at Carson. The work "city" rarely appeared in contemporary government reports.

While I am at it, let me mention what I consider to be one of the most curious terms in numismatics, one used to describe particularly

A Coin by Any Other Name

elusive coins, that being *excessively rare*. To me, *excessively rare* means *too rare*—or rarer than it should be or can be. I prefer *exceedingly rare*. However, I note in my own firm's catalogues the phrase "excessively rare" has crept in here and there over the years—but such instances were coins catalogued by other members of the firm.

I have even heard arguments on the definition of what a coin is. Does a coin have to be legal tender and of a specific denomination, or can a coin be something else? For example, is a privately-issued copper Civil War token a coin or is it not? Can it be owned by a *coin* collector, or is the owner referred to as something else entirely—a *token* collector.

Usually when writing an article I try to draw some conclusions, but the present discussion is an exception. I simply raise points. Fred Schwan advises me that the Numismatic Literary Guild is endeavoring to create a style guide to be used by all in the hobby—or is it an *industry* because some call it that?

As is the case for preferences for religion, politics, and even the desirability of smooth over crunchy peanut butter, there may not be a wrong or right answer to many of the things I have brought up.

B. Max Mehl: The 1913 Nickel Man

by Thomas S. LaMarre   RCR 64 1987

Fort Worth wasn't exactly the coin collectors' capital in 1900. Yet a shoe clerk turned coin dealer put the city on the numismatic map and made coins big business—really big, as Ed Sullivan would say. There was a bit of show biz in B. Max Mehl, too.

Born in Lithuania in 1884, Mehl was brought to the United States at the age of nine. Before long he was collecting coins and swapping duplicates with other numismatists. While working as a shoe clerk, Mehl started a part-time coin business in 1900 and issued his first coin circular in 1903. Then came his first fixed price list in 1904 and his first auction sale in 1906.

In July 1906 Mehl gave up the shoe business in order to concentrate on coins. In an ad in *The Numismatist* he announced, "With pleasure I beg to advise my friends and patrons that I now devote all my time to the coin business. Before it was only a 'sideline' with me but thanks to the esteemed patronage favored me by many of the 'faithful,' my business grew to such an extent that I was obliged to abandon all other interests and devote all my time to serving those who find me worthy of a share of their esteemed numismatic favors.

"I only wish to state that I am in a position to serve you most satisfactory *(sic)* and your favor will certainly be appreciated. I shall try my very utmost to merit same. Kindly let me hear from you whether buyer or seller. Give me a chance to *show you* how nice I can take care of your favors. Your want list will have my best attention. B. Max Mehl,

Numismatist, PO Box 826, Fort Worth, Texas."

By 1908 he was publishing *Mehl's Numismatic Monthly*, in which he boasted, "As to the publisher I only wish to mention my success in the numismatic field. Within less than two years I have succeeded in obtaining a good share of the confidence and patronage of the numismatists of the country. My sales in 1907 aggregate $25,000. And the prospects of the future are very promising indeed." Mehl was never one to show modesty.

In subsequent years he had cause to brag, too. Most of the United States rarities passed through his hands at least once. In 1946 he sold an 1894-S dime (one of only 24 minted) for $2,325—peanuts now, but big money in the 1940s. The same year, Mehl also sold the Stickney specimen 1804 dollar for $10,500, the highest price ever realized by a coin at that time. There must have been gasps of disbelief from oldtimers who had been astounded when Mehl sold a Brasher doubloon for $3,000 in 1922 (the Ten Eyck sale). Another rarity auctioned by the Texas dealer was the finest known specimen of the 1793 Liberty Cap cent. It realized $2,000.

No wonder Mehl attracted the leading collectors as his clients. He handled the Albert A. Grinnell paper money collection ($39,000), the Waldo Newcomer Collection ($220,000) and the William C. Atwater Collection ($153,514). The "Royal Sale," consisting of coins from the collections of King Farouk and Dr Allenburger, brought $116,467.

However, retail sales from the Mehl building were his bread and butter, thanks to advertising. Recalling the early days of his coin business, Mehl said, "I noticed that no effort was being made by anyone to popularize coin collecting and to create new collectors. The idea occurred to me to try advertising in general publications. My first 'large' advertisement appeared in Colliers—a five-liner at the huge cost, at least to me then, of $12.50."

Mehl wisely realized that it was necessary to popularize coin collecting in order to make the hobby big business. Consequently, his goal was not only to sell coins but to "sell" coin collecting. Running ads in numismatic publications was not enough; Mehl also advertised in general interest magazines like *The American Weekly* and *The Saturday Evening Post*.

When commercial radio began, Mehl was quick to see its possibilities. In an ad in the June 1933 issue of *The Numismatist*, he proclaimed, "Coins by radio... Being aware of changing conditions, and although I spent over $50,000 this season for magazine and newspaper advertising, I am now entering the radio field.

"Since January 8th, when my first broadcast appeared over WMAQ Chicago, and which proved very successful, I have had numismatic programs on the air on no less than 50 stations, including all of the larger broadcasting stations in the country, at a cost of over $14,000.

"Radio advertising is of such a nature that, besides these broadcasts proving of value to my own business, it is proving of inestimable value in increasing the value of every collection as well as creating business for all numismatic dealers.

"And, incidentally, of course, this is one of the many reasons why my sales are so successful, and why I can afford to pay more for your coins: I have the recognized largest distribution as well as the largest source of supply."

Mehl claimed that he was never burned in any of his purchases. "I am one of those who hold that nothing can be successfully counterfeited," he explained. "And my experience has tended to prove it. Of course, you will understand that one must know how to tell the true from the counterfeit. It is a matter of knowledge. I have never been taken in by a counterfeit, even of a coin of a country or age in which I am not particularly an authority. No man, to be sure, can be an absolute authority with respect to all coins. There are specialists in this business as in all others. I am supposed to be an authority on American coins. There are authorities in the coinage of other countries. If I am not sure about a coin, I always know when to find a man who can be sure about it. No coin or note can be counterfeited successfully. I mean it cannot be counterfeited so that an expert cannot tell it from the true."

A typical Mehl ad stated, "Right now I will pay $50 for 1913 Liberty Head nickels (not Buffalo), $100 for 1894 dimes, "S"mint, $8 for 1853 quarters, No Arrows, $200 each for 1884 and 1885 silver trade dollars, 10 cents each for 1912 "S" mint nickels..." The catch? People had to buy Mehl's *Star Rare Coin Book* at one dollar per copy to know which coins were valuable. In addition, Mehl offered an illustrated coin folder for only four cents.

The ads never brought in a 1913 Liberty nickel—at least not at $50. But they did contribute to Mehl's wealth. A million copies of the *Star* catalogue were sold. To keep up with the demand, the Mehl building was equipped with its own printing shop. Not everyone liked what they read. Many newcomers to coin collecting were disappointed to find there was a difference between an 1885 trade dollar and an 1885 Morgan dollar, or a 1913 Buffalo nickel and a 1913 Liberty nickel. While some people may have felt victimized, though, others discovered a new hobby.

Mehl dealt with beginners and advanced collectors alike. He tried for years to get Colonel E.H.R. Green as a customer and finally succeeded (Green's purchases were legendary; he owned all five 1913 Liberty nickels). Another one of Mehl's customers was Amon G. Carter.

But Mehl himself gave up coin collecting when he established his business. "A man cannot collect that in which he deals," he said. "It is my business to buy and sell coins, so I am not a coin collector." Instead, he specialized in autographs.

Mehl sold more than coins; he sold an image. Ads pictured the Mehl building, Mehl standing in front of his luxurious home, or other scenes intended to depict the dealer as a coin tycoon.

In 1950 Mehl published a small booklet titled *Recognition of 50 Years of Numismatic Service,* which marked his golden anniversary as a coin dealer. It was a tribute booklet, full of the kind of testimonials that he used in magazine ads. Mehl was acknowledged as the dean of American coin dealers, a role that he accepted as a matter of record.

In 1949 Mehl was the subject of an article in *The Saturday Evening Post*—no doubt he was delighted to get some free space in the magazine which had featured so many of his ads. For his efforts to promote coin collecting, he was awarded an honorary membership in the American Numismatic Association in 1950.

Mehl's ads are now yellowed and the prices in the *Star* catalogue look ridiculously cheap. Fort Worth's famous numismatist, who died in 1957 at age 74, probably wouldn't believe the prices in the current edition of the *Guide Book of United States Coins.* But he was the one who helped make those valuations possible by popularizing the hobby.

A New Grading System

| Some Whimsy by Fred Schwan RCR 64 1987 |

Fred Schwan, one of the hobby's most respected numismatic writers, recently sent us this article, which appeared in Numismatic News, *October 7, 1986. We thought readers would enjoy this satirical commentary on the current grading situation.*

Grading continues to be the greatest problem in numismatics. We have been grappling with the grading of coins, medals and even paper money for several years, but the grading of coin bags has not been examined in the numismatic media.

I grade bags by an informal system which is analogous to the Sheldon-ANA MS (mint state) system. I call this the B.S. system which, of course, means the Bag State system.

In the old days bags were simply graded as New or Used. Those were also the days when there was very little competition for even the most desirable bags. There were few collectors and they were very quiet in their quest for historic bags.

Today, however, the demand far exceeds the supply. This is particularly true of early, classic bags. What collector can resist a bag of CC, New Orleans, or even San Francisco, Denver, or Philadelphia silver dollars?

This is in spite of the fact that as recently as 1963 any collector could have acquired a beautiful BS-60 or better bag (along with 1,000 silver dollars) directly from local banks. Just think, if you had ordered a bag in

1963 for $1,000 you could have spent or returned the coins and kept the bag for free. You could now probably make $20 on the deal!

Indeed, even without compounding the rate of return, profit would be infinite since the cost was zero! This appreciation could be made to appear very attractive in an investment bulletin!

Bags such as these are very interesting and desirable because of the great interest which has been generated in silver dollars. Just as with their contents, silver dollar bags are popular but not terribly rare.

When Saint-Gaudens $20 gold pieces were being actively promoted as investment items in recent months, I received an interesting brochure from an investment firm.

The firm's brochure proclaimed that they had been very fortunate in purchasing intact an original mint bag of these double eagles. It then went on about what a unique opportunity this was to purchase one or more of these coins. I thought it was a unique opportunity to obtain an interesting bag!

I wrote to the firm about acquiring the bag, but I never received a reply. It probably had received many requests for the bag and had sold it.

How many double eagles were in a bag? I do not know. If there were 1,000 pieces in a bag, this one example probably establishes that bags are 1,000 times as scarce as are gold pieces. This and many other important aspects of the history of mint bags in American numismatic history are still shrouded in mystery.

When were the first bags used? Who were the designers of the various type bags that have been used since bags were first used? What is the historical development of the mint coin bag? What political maneuvering surrounded the replacement of coin kegs with coin bags? Do hoards of bags exist? I have heard a rumor that a prominent East Coast dealer is preparing a manuscript which will answer these and many other important questions about mint bags. The title of the book is going to be something like *The History of United States Coins as Described by United States Mint Bags*. Unfortunately, I cannot confirm this rumor of an approaching publication, but such a book is certain to be a bestseller.

Recently some interesting American bags appeared in two foreign auctions. It was these auctions which pointed out the need for clarification of the grading standards.

The first bag which I purchased was a 1944 San Francisco Mint bag for Australian threepence pieces. Its grade was not described in the

A New Grading System

catalogue but I bid on it assuming that it was in less that BS-60 condition. I won the lot and was well pleased with the bag, which I would now grade EF-40.

When the next auction catalogue arrived, another bag was included. It was a Denver Mint bag for 1942 Australian sixpence pieces. This lot was also without description of grade. I bid with the same assumptions. When the bag arrived, I was disappointed in it. I now grade it only VF-20.

Grading bags is a science even less refined than grading coins and paper money. There are *many* interesting facets to consider in grading bags.

First there is the basic bag, which is subject to routine wear as bags are shipped from the mint and between banks. In addition to routine wear, the bags are frequently marred if dropped when full of coins. I call these serious mars "pallet marks."

The markings on bags, which are applied by stencilling, are very important to the value and grade of a bag. These markings are exactly analogous to the designs on a coin, and their clarity and brightness are critical.

Unfortunately, markings were not uniformly applied but rather varied from mint to mint and from year to year Collectors must therefore know the characteristics of original markings and evaluate the markings with respect to the state of preservation rather than mere appearance.

One of the interesting aspects of bag grading is that most bags have been sewn shut and then opened at the top. Bags that have been sewn and never been opened must still have the coins therein. These coins make storing of bag collections difficult. I do not know of any bag albums which also accommodate coins by the thousand.

Bags which were not issued may actually be specimen or even pattern bags. The standards below apply equally to these pieces, but collectors should know that many veteran hobbyists frown on the merit of having such bags in a collection, because they have never been sewn shut.

In some cases, bags were not opened carefully and the opening may be frayed. Bags may even have been reused unofficially and resewn.

You will notice that I have only included descriptions on seven Bag States, but I expect to be able to expand this system to include at least 11 grades of Bag State.

Unfortunately I have not been able to define a BS-61, -62, -68 or -69. I am, however, attempting to assemble a reference set that can be used in establishing definitions.

With this introduction I will discuss the grade descriptions I have developed.

BS-70: Bags must be perfect to be in this grade. They must be original, never used. If the bag was issued, it must still contain the coins and the sewing must still be intact.

BS-67: If the bag has been used, the open edge may not have any fraying.

BS-66: The bag may have been used, but there should be no fraying. It may have no wear or pallet marks. The markings must be perfect.

BS-65: The markings must be perfect, there may be no wear or pallet marks. The open end of the bag may not be frayed.

BS-64: Bags in this grade do not quite meet the standards described for BS-65 but is better than BS-63 below.

BS-63: The bag may not have any wear but a few pallet marks may be present. Fraying at the open end at the seam may not extend more than one inch from the seam.

BS-60: This is the typical grade for an Uncirculated bag. Although no wear is allowed, there will probably be pallet marks and compression marks on the inside of the bag. The stencil markings may not be worn but may have slight fading from exposure to light.

AU-58: This bag is better than AU-55 described below, but does not meet the standards necessary for BS-60 above. The bag should not have been laundered. Fraying may be showing up to as much as one-half of the open end but the fraying may not be more than one-quarter inch in length.

AU-55: Traces of wear are evident on the corners of the bag. Fraying may extend around the entire mouth of the bag. This bag may have been laundered and pressed, but starch or artificial substances may not remain in the bag. If it has been pressed, no iron marks may be visible under magnified examination.

AU-50: Wear will be evident at the corners and around the bag.

EF-45: All edges of the bag will show wear. Fraying around the mouth will be complete, but threads will not come loose.

EF-40: Even wear will show on the obverse and reverse sides of the bag. The printing may be faded and show very light wear, but must be

A New Grading System

bright.

VF-30: This is the grade of the typical bag that has seen moderate use. The bag may have been washed several times. The markings will show weakening, but will be complete. Fraying will be complete with threads up to one inch in length.

VF-20: This bag is better than F-12 below, but does not meet the standards for VF-30 above.

F-12: This bag has seen considerable wear. The legends are readable, but are weakening from repeated washings. If it has not been washed it should be!

VG-8: This bag has probably been used several times. The opening may show damage from multiple openings and closings. The lettering will be weak but fully legible.

G-4: The smallest letters on the bag may be illegible, but the major legends must be readable and the bag fully identifiable. Fraying will be considerable at the mouth. The bag may have been repaired by minor stitching of the seams.

AG-3: The lettering is well worn, but the bag is identifiable. The bag may have been patched or holes sewn shut.

Collectors must also be wary of altered, counterfeit, and fantasy bags. Bogus stenciling can be applied to common bags to give them the appearance of scarce bags.

Faded stencilling may be repaired by skillful but deceitful collectors. In this regard it is handy to know that colored marking pens were not available to the public before 1950.

Coin bags may be subject to "doctoring" in an attempt to improve the apparent grade of a bag. Certainly bags do not lend themselves to whizzing or polishing, however, bags that are available for collectors have frequently been laundered and they may have even been starched and ironed.

Genuine bags can be altered to make them appear to be more desirable. Collectors should be wary of anyone offering a bag purported to have held 1913 Liberty Head five-cent pieces. In this case there is a very high probability that the bag was actually for Buffalo five-cent pieces. This is certainly true if it is a Denver or San Francisco bag.

Another bag that is open to doubt is the one for Philadelphia 1922 cents. Bags for 1944 Denver cents are often altered to resemble 1914 Denver bags.

Collectors need an official standard in order to properly classify their collections. Once a standard B.S. grading system has been instituted, it will be an easy matter for price guides to simply add a new column to each coin listing for the B.S. bag for that respective coin.

Short listings of this type will suffice until demand allows publication of a separate price publication for bags.

This guide has been useful to me in cataloguing my collection of mint bags. It is hoped that it will be useful to other collectors as well. It is the best we have until the American Numismatic Association adopts official standards for the grading of bags and begins authenticating and grading bags.

If ANACS does not include bags in its service and adopt the B.S. grading system, commercial services may begin processing bags and ANACS will lose its leadership position in grading numismatic items.

[Editor's note: *As you might suspect by now, B.S. is an important part of the "science" of grading!*]

The Mint's Balancing Act

by Thomas S. LaMarre   RCR 66 1987

File marks on early United States coins bear mute testimony to the adjustment of planchet weight by hand. By 1876, however, gold pieces and trade dollars were the only coins to be singly weighed and adjusted by hand.

Realizing that the adjustment process was time consuming and costly, Congress allowed the fractional coins' legal deviation from standard weight to be three times larger than the deviation that was permissible for gold pieces. The law therefore implied that fractional coins were to be adjusted by machinery. Accordingly, the Mint used a drawbench to insure uniform thickness of the rolled strips from which the blanks for fractional coins were cut.

Because a small percentage of coins slightly beyond legal tolerance for weight escaped observation and passed into circulation, Director of the Mint H.R. Linderman reported in 1876: ". . .as a safeguard against any pieces being made and issued which might be outside the legal tolerance for weight, an appropriation was obtained at the last session of Congress for the purpose of procuring automatic assorting and adjusting balances, to be employed in testing the weight of the subsidiary coin. Arrangements have been made for importing these balances, and they will be placed in operation at an early day"

Linderman ordered two machines from Seyss & Co. of Atzegersdorf, Switzerland for use at the Philadelphia Mint, and one machine manufactured by Napier & Son of London for the San Francisco Mint.

The machines that were imported from Austria were put into constant use, primarily for half dollar planchets, and the results were "very satisfactory," according to Linderman. They had a combined capacity of 160 blanks per minute.

On October 16,1877 O.C. Bosbyshell, coiner at the Philadelphia Mint, wrote:

"In response to the inquiry of the Director in his letter of the 15th instant desiring a report "as to the result of the use of the Seyss automatic assorting machine," I have the honor to state that the two machines are in good working order and very satisfactory. The last one received came arranged for the reception of the blanks before milling, as ordered, and the first one has been altered by the machinists of this mint so as to do the same thing. This alteration enables us to have all heavy pieces that may be detected reduced by hand to the limit allowed by law.

"The machines have developed the fact that any failure on the part of the draw-benches to properly adjust the strips is quickly and positively detected.

"We are using these machines only on the half dollar coinage, as the delay in passing the other denominations of subsidiary coin through is so great that we cannot afford to lose the time.

"In view of this I would most respectfully recommend, at the proper time, the purchase of at least two additional machines in order to enable us to use them upon all the subsidiary coin.

"I might add in conclusion that I consider these machines essentially necessary to guard against the issue of coins outside the legal limit of tolerance for weight. So far as my experience goes, a machine adjustment—that is, the drawbench—is not sufficiently certain to secure a positive adherence to the requirements of the law in all cases."

Frank X. Cicott, coiner at the San Francisco Mint, expressed a slightly different view regarding the Napier machine. On October 20, 1877 he wrote:

"In accordance with instructions received from the director, I herewith submit to you the result of the experiments with the Napier automatic balance recently received at this mint.

"Its present capacity is only for weighing blanks of the denominations of half eagles, quarter eagles, and dimes, though with a little alteration it could be made to also adjust quarter dollars. Experiments have been made with both quarter eagles and dimes, and we find that the greatest number of pieces that it will weigh with positive accuracy is 25 per minute.

"I cannot see unless the coinage of small gold is to be very much increased, any great benefit to be derived from the use of a machine of the small capacity of the one received, as we do not devote more than one-half day in each year to the adjustment of half and quarter eagles, while there is no difficulty whatever in adjusting quarter dollars and dimes within the limit at the draw-bench in the cutting room.

"The only machine of the kind, in my opinion, that would be particularly useful to us in this mint would be one of sufficiently large size to weigh double eagles and trade dollars, and with a speed equal to about 50 pieces per minute; such a machine, if one could be constructed, would undoubtedly result in the saving of considerable time and labor, though it would require at least 10 balances of the above-named capacity to perform the work of this department. I will say, in conclusion, that I am convinced that the machine will perform all that is represented or claimed for it by the manufacturers, and that it will be quite valuable to us as a test machine for testing blanks as they come from the cutting room."

Linderman recommended in his annual report that "an appropriation should be procured to supply the mints with a sufficient number of these machines to test all the blanks for fractional coins."

Mechanization was imperative because the mints' employees were already overworked. Congress had directed that the mints be operated at full capacity and Linderman wrote that although "the employees have been required to work, in addition to the regular day's work of eight hours, as many extra hours as they could endure, not a single word of complaint has been heard from any source."

Results of special test assays of United States coins taken from deliveries at the mints in each month during the fiscal year which ended June 30, 1877 found double eagles ranging from 515.68 to 516.20 grains (the standard weight was 516 grains); dimes from 38.20 to 38.80 grains (38.58 standard); half dollars from 192.45 to 193.75 grains (192.9 standard); and trade dollars from 419.30 to 420 grains (420 standard).

Accurate weight and fineness had always been a major concern of the Mint and the meeting of the annual Assay Commission became an important tradition. The February 1941 issue of *The Numismatist* said:

"The numismatists of America should consider the second Wednesday in February a holiday, for this is the date prescribed by law for the meeting of the annual Assay Commission each year at the US Mint in Philadelphia.

"The traditional ceremony of the "trial of the pyx" is a very serious matter, as for the past two years there have been record productions of coinage, so that the work of the commission has not been as perfunctory as it has been in times past when smaller coinages were struck.

"The Assay Commission is appointed each year by the president, with the following three members in regular attendance: The judge of the District Court for the eastern district of Pennsylvania, the comptroller of the currency, and the chief assayer. These three officials meet with such other persons as the president may designate, and are termed Assay Commissioners. The provisions for the present commission are contained in the revised statutes, Sec. 3547. The commission was created in 1792 and is one of the oldest government institutions.

"Following are the details and methods of the duties of the commission prepared in advance of the meeting:

"At the United States mints at Philadelphia, Denver, and San Francisco not less than one silver coin of every 2,000 delivered from the coining room must be reserved for test by the commission to determine whether the coins conform to legal requirements as to weight and fineness. The sample coins are required to be sealed and carefully preserved in a "pyx" under the joint care of the superintendent and assayer for delivery to the commission.

"The word "pyx" in the law is derived from "pyx-chest," a receptacle for new English coins once kept in the Chapel of the Pyx in Westminster Abbey, London. For the 1940 test, the 79,847 coins were reserved at the three United States coinage mints and are now assembled at the Philadelphia Mint in the manner prescribed by law. The coins are carefully guarded in the "pyx" at Philadelphia awaiting trial by the commission.

"Mrs. Nellie Taylor Ross, director of the Mint, will be present at the Philadelphia ceremony. Dr. L.J. Briggs, director of the Bureau of Standards, will carry with him from Washington the official weights of the Bureau of the Mint, which have been calibrated at the Bureau of Standards for the annual test of the coinage.

"The law specifies that sample coins deposited by superintendents of the coinage mints for the annual test shall "be sealed by the superintendent in an envelope on which shall be inscribed the place of coinage, the date, number, and amount of delivery, the number and denominations of pieces enclosed, and a certificate signed by the superintendent and assayer that the facts are as stated."

The sealed parcels, the law provides, shall be deposited in the pyx, designated for the purpose at each mint, to be kept under the joint care of the superintendent and assayer and be secured so that neither can have access to its contents without the presence of the other. The law directs that the reserved pieces from the coinage of mints other than the Philadelphia Mint, shall, in their sealed envelopes, be transmitted quarterly by express or registered mail to the Mint at Philadelphia, where they shall be carefully preserved in a pyx under the joint care of the superintendent and assayer, for delivery to the annual Assay Commission.

"That great historical import has always been attached to the appointment of the members of the commission is evidenced by the names of several illustrious appointees. Thomas Jefferson, John Marshall, and Alexander Hamilton have at one time served as members."

On February 9, 1977, in an economy move by President Jimmy Carter, public members were dropped from the annual Assay Commission. H.R. Linderman, who took great pains to insure the Mint's accuracy, would have found that hard to believe.

The Coin Market is Alive and Well

by Dr. Joel J. Orosz

Our readers will enjoy the following article by Dr. Joel J. Orosz, certainly one of the most astute observers in today's numismatic world. Dr. Orosz has appeared in our columns before, and he is also well known as the author of the book, The Eagle That is Forgotten.

In the autumn of 1990, as the leaves fluttered to the ground, something else was dropping: the value of slabbed coins. In fact, price trends for these coins were dropping more like rocks than leaves. As the bottom fell out of the speculative portion of the coin market, legions of dazed and battered investors could be heard moaning, as they unloaded their coins at fire-sale prices, that the market was as dead as a mackerel. Meanwhile, observing from the sidelines, many collectors could hardly suppress their glee. The meltdown of the overheated slab market, they hoped, would eliminate the investment virus from the numismatic system, and the golden age of coin collecting would be reborn. If they were to have theme songs, the investors would be warbling "The Party's Over," while the collectors would be crooning "Ding, Dong, the Witch is Dead."

While it may be impolite to cut in on the choir, it seems that both the funeral dirge and the victory march are very premature. Although many collectors and investors do not remember them, there have been several market crashes in the coin hobby before the crash of 1990. All of these hard times offer lessons to us, if only we would take the time to learn them. Since I have been around for awhile, the current ruckus reminds me of the story about the child who burst out of Sunday school one Sabbath morning, dashed up to his mother, and announced breathlessly, "Holy Moses! Jonah's been eaten by a whale!" Market ups and downs, like Jonah's plight, are old news by now, for there have been booms and busts ever since there have been markets. True, it has been quite some time—at least a decade—since the coin market has gone South.

But the crash of 1990 is, in many ways, just an instant replay of 1980, 1973, 1964, or previous market dips in the fifties, forties, and thirties. And after each and every one of these jolts, the coin market bounced back at least as good as before.

It might be useful, therefore, to take a moment to think about the lessons of history. After reviewing the nine lessons which follow, I think that you will see that for the marketplace in coins, as for Mark Twain, it is truly the case that "the reports of my death are greatly exaggerated." And, if you will pardon the expression, you can bet your bottom dollar that when a strong market for coins returns in the future, investors will be back in force. But enough prelude. The lessons of history await.

Lesson #1: All Booms Have Busts

When studying any market, always remember "Sinatra's Law": booms and busts are like love and marriage—you can't have one without the other. "Sinatra's Law" holds for *every* market, from the New York Stock Exchange to the neighborhood lemonade stand. This is simple, common-sense, what-goes-up-must-come-down stuff. Why is it then, that so many investors were shocked when their bubble burst? Most of the blame can be placed upon the tidal wave of hype that has issued forth from the investment-oriented dealers. You know the drill: the market is red-hot. . . buy now—coins are going out of sight. . . double your money before lunch. . . and so on, ad nauseam. Thousands of investors swallowed this puff pastry of promotion in a single gulp. So, came the deluge, these people were caught flat-footed. Many lost money they could not afford to lose, and more than a few lost all interest in ever buying another coin. It is a shame, but it might not have happened had they remembered that every numismatic "Roaring Twenties" is followed by its own version of the Great Depression. This is the first great lesson of history.

Lesson #2: All Busts (Eventually) Have Booms

There is, however, a silver lining. If every boom is followed by a bust, it is also true every bust is followed by some sort of boom. Those who are patient are usually rewarded when the market regains its equilibrium. The lesson here is that those who are in the game for the long term usually do well—but those who chase short term gains usually lose their shirts—and frequently their pants and their long johns too. As one of my math teachers was fond of remarking, "Everything goes around in cycles." The great robber baron, J. Pierpont Morgan, once put this in more economic terms. A gentleman asked him what the stock market was going to do, to which Morgan replied, "It will fluctuate."

Alas, lessons like these are too often lost on most numismatists. They think in a linear fashion; if the market is rising, it will keep rising in a straight line, forever. If the market is falling, it will drop like a boulder without ceasing. Thus, booms give rise to euphoria, and busts spawn despair, but neither produces much common sense. Well, whether in boom or bust, here is a piece of common sense to remember; if you are distressed about the current state of the coin market, wait a few months. Quite likely, it will be very different then.

Lesson #3: The Market Always Survives

As the debris from the investment coin market crashes to earth, it is hard—sometimes all but impossible—to remember the third lesson of history: Provided that the market has fundamental *value*, it will always survive the crash.

Probably the best example of this is the New York Stock Exchange. American history is littered with terrible speculative "busts" that, when they happened, seemed irreversible: The panic of 1837, the collapse of 1893, the Great Depression of 1929. In every case, however, the market had fundamental value: The stocks being traded were in companies that mostly were profitable and growing enterprises. As a result, once the panic subsided, the money flowed back to the market. This happened again in 1987 and 1989, when the fear spawned by stock market crashes quickly dissipated, and price levels bounced back in a matter of months.

The key question, then, is whether the coin market has fundamental value. Of course, with the exception of trade dollars, every U.S. coin in every collection is worth its face value, but that is cold comfort to those who have paid huge premiums for their coins. The good news is that there is a vast safety net strung out above the face-value floor; a net made of millions of coin collectors. When the coin market crashes, when speculators sell out and hide under the rocks, the collector is there to steady the market. How this happens is a fascinating story in itself.

Collectors, you see, are in for the long haul. They buy slowly, but steadily, with surplus funds. In other words, they don't bet the rent money that the coins will rise in value overnight.

Instead, they make frequent smaller purchases as they can afford to do so. When a bull market drives the prices of the coins too high, the collectors simply stop buying. When that happens, investors see that the short-term gains they have been chasing are disappearing. So, the speculators panic, start selling in a lather, and the market crashes; crashes, that is, until the prices get low enough to be attractive to collectors who continue to buy steadily over the long haul. Collectors then begin buying in the depressed areas, and their purchases put an end to the crash. After collectors stabilize the situation, investors rush back, overheat the market once more, and then collectors pull the plug again by halting their buying. And so it goes.

Earlier, I compared collectors to a safety net; it might be better to compare them to a thermostat that promotes long-term growth while preventing the coin price structure from getting too high—or too low. As long as we have millions of collectors who are long-term buyers, the coin market has fundamental value. We do have millions of them right now, so I can confidently predict that the coin market will recover from the crash of 1990. It should give us a chill, however, to think of what would happen if the collector base dissolved. In that case, you would see a lot of old and rare coins in the tills of the local gas stations and supermarkets, for that is exactly what coins, without collectors, are worth; face value.

Lesson #4: Investors Never Learn—And Always Return

With a few notable exceptions (the contrarians, about whom we will hear more later), investors never learn. The investor, you see, tends to be a herd animal. He loves to be a part of the crowd. In numismatics, he displays this herding instinct by buying what is "hot." These coins, of course, tend to be items that are already near the top of their price cycle, and due for a fall. Buying overpriced coins is exactly what a savvy investor should *not* do, of course, but herding investors, alas, are not very savvy. That is why they follow their herding instincts to complete disaster when the market turns sour. Everyone else seems to be selling, so they are determined to sell, too. When most everyone is selling, however, those few who are still buying are collectors and contrarians—and they are paying only what they think the coins are worth—usually a few cents on the dollar that the investor paid for them.

Whole herds of speculators, therefore, are regularly buying high and selling low. Most financial experts agree that this is generally not the way in which great fortunes are made. In fact, you can quite literally say that most investors follow the herd for all they are worth. Moreover, history suggests that speculators are slow to learn. I have personally witnessed the coin market crashes of 1973, 1980, and now, 1990. In each case, investors made the same mistakes that laid low their predecessors in the previous panic. Worse than that, it was often the identical investors getting burned in the identical way time after time. Same mistake, different crash, same result; lost money. So, you can bank on it; despite the crash of 1990, investors will be back, and ready to be shorn again at the next shearing.

Lesson #5: Collectors and Contrarians Always Win

As the old adage goes, "for every winner, there is a long line of losers." If legions of investors have been the losers, collectors, and that rare-bird investor, the contrarian, are the winners. We have already seen how collectors win. They buy slowly, but steadily, through good times and bad, paying for coins based on their judgment of the coin's real value. I don't know of anyone who has done this and lost money over the long term, unless they were buying counterfeits.

The contrarians, on the other hand, are investors who deliberately avoid the herd. They quietly purchase coins when markets are bad, and just as quietly sell when markets are good. Perhaps the most notable contrarian was the stock market wizard Bernard Baruch, whose formula for success on Wall Street was simple; "I buy when everyone else is selling, and sell when everyone else is buying." The oldest advice in the world, of course, is to "buy low and sell high," but precious few have the courage to actually do it.

So, in every numismatic panic, the collectors and the contrarians calmly count their winnings, while the speculators trample each other in a mad and money-losing rush to the exits. How ironic it is that investors—people who are in numismatics for the expressed purpose of making money—are the ones who always take the biggest bath come the day of reckoning. Some would call it poetic justice.

Lesson #6: Not All of the Market Crashes

Just about every numismatic writer—including me—is addicted to the sweeping generalization. We all say "the coin market" as if there were a single coin market that rose and fell all at once. This, of course, is poppycock. The "coin market" is really a patchwork quilt composed of dozens of smaller markets, ranging from familiar subjects like Peace dollars to obscure specialties like museum admission tokens. To be sure, some of these markets rise and fall together, but others are completely unaffected by what any other portion on the market is doing. Some examples will serve to show how this works.

In autumn 1936, the booming market in commemorative coins suddenly went sour, but most of the rest of the coin market stayed on an even keel. Twenty-one years later in 1957, the big bull market in Proof sets took a pounding, but other areas, notably late-date Uncirculated rolls, remained hot. Even in the worst slumps that the coin market has suffered—1964-1966 and 1980-1982—there were pockets of great strength.

Today, even as purveyors of Morgan dollars and 20th-century gold cry over their balance sheets, those who deal in large cents, Lincoln cents, Capped Bust halves, and many other areas gloat over their receipts. In fact, copper coins are the closest thing in numismatics to a "recession-proof" area. Since these market segments are dominated by collectors, there is strong demand for them no matter whether other segments go up or down. Clearly, then, not all of the market has crashed; in fact, some parts of it are doing better than ever.

Lesson #7: Now is the Time to Buy

At the risk of sounding like the investment gurus who are always urging people to buy! buy! buy!, I will tell you that yet another lesson of history is that, for the investment coin portion of the market, anyway, *now* is the time to buy. Just after a bust, prices are depressed, and dealers are eager to turn over inventories that are, as they say, "eating them alive." Buyers will find it is simply better to deal with merchants who are desperate to make a sale than those who can't keep up with the demand.

It is easy to wish that you could travel in time back to the "trough" years of 1965 or 1981 to get bargains, but in fact there is no need. It appears that 1991 will be a "trough" year as well for investment series like Morgan dollars and 20th-century gold. In these areas, numismatists with want lists would be wise to heed the old adage: "There's no time like the present."

Lesson #8: Knowledge is All-Important

It was Francis Bacon who said, "knowledge is power." As far as I know, no one has ever said "ignorance is power," yet all too many people in numismatics act as if they believe this maxim to be true. For some reason, when buying coins, a lot of people plunge in without stopping to learn even the most basic information about them. Oddly enough, most of these folks would never dream of buying a car without first taking a test drive, or putting money into a house without first inspecting it. Yet these same people are willing to spend thousands of dollars without knowing a blessed thing about the coins they are buying. Speculators seem especially prone to this temptation, and history shows us that every crash includes as its victims thousands of would-be high rollers who "knew" about coins only what slick-talking shills from some boiler-room operation told them.

As sad as it is, it is not as if these unfortunates had not been warned. Time and again, speculators have been admonished, cajoled, begged, exhorted, and even bribed into making a study of their area of numismatic interest. They almost never do, usually claiming that books are too expensive to buy and too time-consuming to read. This is just about as logical as saying that in order to save time and money, you won't hire a lawyer to defend you against a murder charge. Most speculators are ignorant because they think they are too busy to become smart. And a direct consequence of that choice is that, sooner or later, they will lose money in the numismatic marketplace.

Past experience tells us that when the market starts to boom again, a fresh crop of speculators will once more line up for the privilege of being beggared at the next market plunge. Although it is probably fruitless to do so, it should be the business of all true numismatists to convince these fresh recruits to *read* about coins. In nearly a quarter of a century in this hobby, I have met literally hundreds of people who bitterly regretted having bought certain coins, but none—not one—who ever regretted buying coin books.

Lesson #9: The Collector is Still King of Numismatics

Judging from the letters to the editor in the popular numismatic press, the *hobby* of coin collecting is dead, or at least dying. It has been overrun by hoards of investors who have "ruined the hobby" by bidding the prices up to absurd levels. And the litany of complaints continues, week after week.

But just when the doomsayers were throwing large shovelfuls of dirt onto the coffin of the collector, he has risen with gusto. While investors did bid up the prices in certain series of coins, these high prices collapsed the moment the collectors decided that such prices made no *numismatic* sense. A case in point was the 1881-S Morgan dollar in MS-65 condition. A year or so ago it would have cost you nearly one thousand dollars to add an example to your collection. Then collectors walked out of the investment orgy, and the price for the 1881-S began a free-fall that didn't stop until the end of 1990, when collectors, attracted by price levels about 20% of this coin's previous level, began to buy them once more.

It is really very simple; speculators in coins arrive, spend a lot of money for a short while, then leave, only to be replaced by others of their ilk. Collectors, by way of contrast, steadily pursue their hobby over a number of years. In fact, the whole idea of investing in coins makes no sense at all unless there is an "end consumer" who wants the coin, and is willing to pay the price for it. Investors certainly are not end consumers—they want to unload their coins, at a profit—and preferably soon. It is collectors who buy coins and hold them because they like them. In truth, collectors create the market for investors.

Thus, the coin market crash of 1990 was an example of the "golden rule" in action—he who has the gold, makes the rules. The market boomed as long as collectors were willing to pay inflated prices for coins. The moment that collectors decided the prices had become too high, the investment market imploded. The collapse was checked when prices fell low enough to make coins attractive once more to collectors. As it happens, the guys who call themselves "market makers" are being just a wee bit presumptuous. The true makers of the coin market are the collectors, and it seems to be equally true to say of collectors, as I have previously said of investors, that "the reports of their death have been greatly exaggerated."

What Are the Lessons of History?

The lessons of history are often harsh, but in numismatics most are very reassuring. First, they tell us that hard times are nothing new—that our fathers and grandfathers weathered the same sort of economic

The Coin Market is Alive and Well

storms that are bedeviling us. In our day, just as it did in theirs, the coin market will recover, stronger than ever. A second important lesson is that investors will not be deterred by their disastrous experience—and will soon be happily pursuing slabbed coins for profit's sake once more. A third vital lesson is that the collector is still king of numismatics, perhaps less often in the spotlight than previously, but still with enough clout to cause coin markets to rise or fall.

Perhaps the most important lesson of them all is that numismatists can either be history's students, or its victims. If we absorb the lessons that history teaches us, we will be prepared for the numismatic markets of the future. To learn these lessons is not necessarily cheap in terms of either time or money. But let me close with an apt thought I saw recently on a bumper sticker: "If you think education is expensive, try ignorance."

A Book From 1889

by Q. David Bowers   1993

The following was written for "The Joys of Collecting" column in COIN WORLD, *1993.*

The other day I parted with the sum of $25 and acquired from Richard Boera a small book titled *The Rare Coins of America*, copyrighted in 1889 by William von Bergen of Boston. The compact, hardbound volume, measuring four by six inches and comprising 114 pages of text and illustrations, was published as a guide to United States and world coins having significant premium values.

For silver dollars, von Bergen stated that he would pay up to $800 for a specimen dated 1804, $100 for a 1794 in Uncirculated grade, and $2 upward for most varieties of Liberty Seated dollars with Uncirculated or Proof finish.

Von Bergen was probably the leading issuer of coin guides in his time. The fact that he was more interested in selling coin books than coins is given in the paragraph below, as also a commentary on ethics (sort of; I refer to "lucky enough"):

"In order to meet the constantly increasing demand for rare coins, a few intelligent and respectable persons (ladies or gentlemen) can have profitable employment in collecting them, and by following the instructions given here can make at least $7 per day, and some day an agent might make $100 or $1000, if he is lucky enough to come across a lot of rare coins of which the owner does not know the value.

But it is easily understood that rare coins are not met with every day, else they would not be rare. A collector ought not to depend upon buying coins to make his pay, but upon selling the Coin Books. If a collector only sells twenty books a day, this will give him a clear profit of $7; and as many as forty are often sold in a day by collectors of some experience. It is a very easy thing to sell the Coin Book in fact, they sell themselves; all you have to do is to tell people what premiums are offered on coins, and they will get so interested in the matter that they will offer to buy a book from you. Any businessman if properly approached will buy a book, as they are a real necessity in any bank or office."

Eventually, von Bergen passed from the earthly scene, but the concept of issuing premium guides did not. In the present century, B. Max Mehl of Fort Worth, Texas, created *The Star Rare Coin Encyclopedia,* of which millions were sold in over 30 editions from the 1900s through the 1950s. Today, copies of the Mehl "encyclopedia" abound, and typically bring $10 to $20 each as curiosities.

This & That

from Rare Coin Review Nos. 85 & 86   1991/1992

THE TEN BEST COIN DESIGNS, in the opinion of well-known numismatic researcher Tom DeLorey, was the subject of a recent article in *COINage* magazine. Tom's choices are as follows: 1915-S Panama-Pacific International Exposition octagonal $50, 1926-1939 Oregon Trail half dollar, 1913-1938 Indian or "Buffalo" nickel, 1836-1839 Gobrecht silver dollar, 1916-1947 Liberty Walking half dollar, 1916-1945 "Mercury" dime, 1796 quarter dollar, 1908-1929 $5, 1907 pattern $20 (Judd-1776), and 1876 pattern silver dollar by William Barber (J-1457). What about the MCMVII (1907) High Relief double eagle? Tom DeLorey had the following to say: "The one coin that almost always leads any list to the most beautiful U.S. coins is the 1907 High-Relief Roman numerals double eagle design by Augustus Saint-Gaudens, and this author will not challenge that designation." He went on to note that while it ranked high in artistic quality, "as a coin design the Saint-Gaudens creation was a flop, requiring five or more strikes per coin to bring up the impossibly High Relief. . . This slowed production to a crawl. . . Therefore, while the High-Relief $20 is arguably the most beautiful U.S. design ever coined, it is also arguably the worst U.S. coin ever designed, requiring replacement with a lesser version after only 11,250 pieces were made. It would have made a great commemorative design."

* * *

LEARN TO ENJOY YOUR COINS: A recent editorial in *Numismatic News* stated in part: "Enjoy your coins—whether they be certified or so-called raw coins. Invest in them because you like their designs, because you enjoy looking at them, because you like old things, because you like history, because you take pride in owning these objects.

"To have a true appreciation for numismatics is the first step toward wise investment of money and time.

"Can you imagine the cynicism of somebody who would invest in a classic painting and have absolutely no appreciation for its non-tangible value as art? Rembrandt didn't paint to make some bonehead rich; he did it for artistic expression.

"Somebody who appreciates the non-tangible value of old coins is going to make all the right tangible moves. That person is going to proceed with care in pursuing something that means more than dollars and cents to him. Just ask any veteran collector who has built a sizeable collection through years of study and genuine interest in the field. His investment will pay off just fine."

* * *

WE HOPE THE RETURN ADDRESS is heaven and not the other place: The following appeared in a recent issue of the American Numismatic Association's "1891 Club Newsletter": "There is still time for you . . . to submit items for the ANA Bicentennial Time Capsule. The capsule will be sealed following the Chicago Centennial Convention [August 1991] and will not be opened until the Chicago Bicentennial Convention in 2091. All items you submit will be loaned to the ANA and be returned to YOU [emphasis ours] following the Bicentennial Convention. Please leave a forwarding address so the items can be returned to you. ANA will pay for the postage."

* * *

GOOD MOTTO: "To save time is to lengthen life"—motto used to advertise the Remington Standard Typewriter in the 1890s.

* * *

KEITH ZANER, in a recent issue of *Coin World,* noted the following (among other things) in his "Trends" column: "Attractive opportunities continue to exist for rare coins at current price levels. This is not to say that even at these levels prices cannot go down even more. However, the levels at which many coins are trading at today make investing in or collecting some coins very desirable. . . The fact is, common date type coins grading MS-63 and higher are attractively priced compared to several years ago. Areas in which the opportunities exist for common dates include MS-63 and MS-64 red and brown Coronet half cents, Coronet cents grading MS-60, MS-63, and MS-64. . . Indian cents grading MS-64 red and brown, and two-cent coins in attractive red and brown MS-64. Other areas of opportunity can be found among common-date, copper-nickel and silver coins . . . Gold coins represent really excellent values now . . . Thus, many collectors and investors are adding these coins to their portfolios at current levels."

* * *

COLLECTORS PRAISE THE MINT: "By far the most notable achievement of the Mint service during the fiscal year. . . was the selection. . . of new designs for the dime, quarter, and half dollar pieces. For the first time in the history of our coinage there are separate designs for each of the three denominations, and their beauty and quality, from a numismatic standpoint, have been highly praised by all having expertise in such matters to whom they have been shown." (From the *Annual Report of the Director of the Mint,* 1916)

* * *

19TH-CENTURY SENTIMENTS as seen on a sheet of uncut stickers, circa 1850, suitable for sealing in a Valentine: "The Wealth of a Cottage Is Love," "A Place in My Memory Dearest," "That Thou Art Lovely, Who'll Deny," "Come, Oh! Come With Me," "Forget and Forgive," "Tarry Not," "In Hope I am Happy," "All's Well That Ends Well," "'Tis the Heart Gives Value to Words," "Do You Ever Think of Me?," "A Letter Softens the Pain of Absence," and "As Innocent as a Lamb." (From *The Ephemera Journal*)

* * *

DAVID GANZ said it in a recent issue of his *The Coin Market Insider's Report:* "Extraordinary book, the two-volume *ANA Centennial History,* written by Q. David Bowers, a truly extraordinary work. His next accomplishments: A massive history of commemoratives *[Commemorative Coins of the United States: A Complete Encyclopedia]* that is destined to be the classic of the field for years to come."

This & That

Thank you, David Ganz!

* * *

COIN PHOTOGRAPHY circa 1900: "According to John Pittman, turn of the century photography was often performed with the coin immersed in water. He recalled duplicating this process with William Clark, assistant curator of the American Numismatic Society, by placing coins in a shallow pan just topped off with water. The coins were then shot outdoors in natural sunlight with an old box camera. The result produced an evenness of texture and avoided glares and shadows. This method is not, however, recommended for photographing books." (From *The Asylum,* Journal of the Numismatic Bibliomania Society, Summer 1991).

* * *

THEFT REPORTED: "Ringling Brothers Barnum & Bailey Circus reported the theft of nearly two tons of elephant dung in Washington, DC. ... The pachyderm poop—representing two weeks' output from 16 elephants—was to be distributed to farmers and gardeners. The circus wouldn't put a value on the filched fertilizer, but said the elephants were busy replacing it." (From *USA Today*)

* * *

BOB KORVER, writing in *The Certified Coin Dealer Newsletter,* had this to say: "The rare coin market of the nineties is developing along two themes. The key concept of buyers inspecting the coins to evaluate appeal is as old a theme as one can find in numismatics. Still, when a potential buyer falls in love with a coin, there remains a question of value. Computers are useful in disseminating prodigious quantities of pricing information, but the information that comes out so rapidly is only as good as the information that goes in. And computers can do very little to help a buyer decide whether he finds the coin appealing."

* * *

IN HIS RECENT CATALOGUE OF THE BAY SALE, Fred Lake had this to say about our auction catalogues (under Lot A42): "(They are) some of the most masterfully done catalogues to be found in numismatics. They are unmatched for depth of description, beautiful photography and content."

* * *

FROM TIME TO TIME we have mentioned the Liberty Seated Collectors Club, a non-profit organization dedicated to Liberty Seated coins from half dimes to dollars. Recently in our mailbox we found *Collective Volume Number 3,* a 469-page hardbound book consisting of selected articles from *The Gobrecht Journal.* It's a great book, and any *Rare Coin Review* readers who are interested in getting one, or learning about the LSCC, are advised to contact the president of the group, John W. McCloskey, 5718 King Arthur Drive, Kettering, OH 45429.

* * *

AN INTERESTING QUOTE from Howard B. Gottlieb, the director of special collections at Boston University's Mugar Memorial Library: "The human animal is a saver by nature. I'm suspicious of people who collect nothing. It shows a lack of interest in life in general." (From the *Boston Sunday Globe Magazine.*)

* * *

AN 1803 SILVER DOLLAR, possibly actually struck in 1804 (for the reported original mintage of 1804 dollars almost certainly involved pieces dated 1803), a beautiful Uncirculated example of the B-5 variety, is the apple of David Pelz's eye. David, a long-term client, lent the piece to *COINage* magazine which featured it on the cover of the November 1991 issue, under the title of "Is This The Real 1804 Dollar?" Congratulations, David, in getting a true numismatic prize.

* * *

SOME DETECTIVE WORK MAY BE NEEDED to figure out who thought of this first, but we couldn't help but be amused

The Numismatist's Topside Companion

by a new Agatha Christie book, entitled *The New Bedside, Bathtub and Armchair Companion to Agatha Christie*. It reminded us of our own *Numismatist's Bedside Companion*—but we have no current plans to issue a *Numismatist's Bathtub Companion*, or an *Armchair Companion*.

* * *

PRICES 50 YEARS AGO: The following quotation is a letter from Thomas L. Elder to *Rare Coin Review* reader Hunter R. Hilton, who today at the age of 82 is as interested in coins as ever: "Dear Mr. Hilton. If you want early cents in Uncirculated condition you will have to pay stiff prices for them. Nobody can furnish such cents cheap. I sold a perfect 1793 cent once for $530 at auction sale, so there's no use talking about an Uncirculated 1793 cent unless you have $150 anyhow for it. Collectors are too fussy and they would get much farther if they weren't so exacting about condition. An Extremely Fine coin is good enough for me. . . No lists, prices change, nobody can issue lists except at enormous retail prices today as prices change overnight. Yours truly, THOMAS L. ELDER (signed).

"P.S.: A Very Fine 1793 cent I offer for only $33.50. Very cheap. Very cheap bargain, you can't buy them for less."

Tom Elder's return address at the time was P.O. Box 1116, Greenville, South Carolina.

In his letter of transmittal, Mr. Hilton, a veteran of collecting for over a half century, also stated this: "*The Buyer's Guide to the Rare Coin Market* that you sent me is the most interesting book about numismatics I have ever read. Thank you very much."

* * *

HOBBIES CAN BE PROFITABLE: From time to time various organizations within coins say that running conventions is not profitable, services should be cut back, etc. We are happy to report that in the related field, the American Theatre Organ Society (to which your editor has belonged for many years; I am the owner of a very small Wurlitzer theatre organ built circa 1919), had in attendance of over 900 people at its latest annual convention, held in San Francisco. After all is said and done, an all-day multi-program was enjoyed by all who attended (which did not include your editor, who was elsewhere at the time) and a profit of $86,000 was realized. And yet no one buys theatre organs for investment; in fact, the word is rarely if ever mentioned at conventions and collector gatherings. The get-togethers are for pure hobby enjoyment—pure fun. Numismatists, take heed!

* * *

SOMETHING TO PONDER: Why is it that we can enjoy listening to a favorite piece of music—a short, popular song as well as a complete symphony—over and over again, year in and year out, without tiring of it; at the same time we can enjoy having a photograph on our desks, or a picture on the wall which is looked at day in and day out for a long period of time. However, put aural and visual things together—such as a cartoon or sound movie—and there is no way that we would want to see it once a month for the next two years or three years or 10 years. Why is it that treats to the ear have a long lifespan and treats to the eyes do as well, but the combination of both is tiring more quickly?

* * *

GINGER RAPSUS, writing in *The Numismatist*, June 1992, gave "fifty reasons why coin collecting is better than baseball card collecting," noting, for example (reason number two): "There are no 'salary surveys' complaining about how much money coin dealers make," and (3) "There are no pre-rookie issues." What caught our eye was number 33: "There is nothing similar to a *Rare Coin Review* or other special catalogue in card collecting." Thanks, Ginger, for the compliment.

The 1964-D Peace Dollar

| by Q. David Bowers | 1993 |

The following was written for "The Joys of Collecting" column in COIN WORLD, *1993.*

Among silver dollars there are many mysteries, not the least of which is this question: Are there any 1964-D Peace dollars in existence?

While doing research for my book, *Silver Dollars and Trade Dollars of the United States: A Complete Encyclopedia,* I had several conversations and exchanges of correspondence about this particular coin. This was not the first time that I checked into the 1964-D, as in the 1970s, when I wrote *Adventures With Rare Coins,* Denver rare coin dealer Dan Brown did some research on my behalf. He related that he had talked with Mrs. Fern Miller, who had been superintendent of the Denver Mint when the 1964-D dollars were made, and learned from her that, as had been the custom throughout the years, mint employees were each allowed to buy two of these new dollars. "Quite a number took advantage of this and bought two pieces each."

Mrs. Miller recalled that later, upon request, many turned the coins back in, but as no record had been kept of the purchasers, there was no way of knowing for sure. What if, in the meantime, an employee had innocently sold one and also did not keep a record of the purchaser?

Especially interested in the 1964-D dollar has been Maryland dealer Robert Cohen, who years ago ran advertisements seeking to find a specimen. To this date, neither Bob Cohen nor any other numismatist to whom I have spoken has seen one of the coins in the flesh. I read with interest the recollections of Denver Mint employee Tito Real, in a recent issue of *Coin World,* that he had seen 1964-D dollars at one time, and that some had been found where they had fallen beneath a radiator at the mint; these were melted.

Recently, I have been given to understand that at least two specimens of the 1964-D may exist today, not coins from the sale to Denver Mint employees, but coins said to have been acquired at the time of striking, by Eva Adams, who was director of the Mint. It was suggested to me that one of these pieces was given to President Lyndon Johnson, and today may well be among his papers and effects. The other is said to have been sold by Director Adams to a well-known Eastern numismatist.

The question of legality has probably kept any surviving pieces "underground." I suggest that if Eva Adams had coins at one time, and disposed of them, these can be legally held today. Somewhat similar is the situation surrounding 1974 aluminum Lincoln cent trial strikings distributed casually by Mint Director Mary Brooks, who then changed her mind, asked for them back, but only a few were returned.

Thousands of different pattern, trial, etc., coins exist today in collections; coins mostly dating from the 19th century, for which no official Mint records of sale exist. Yet, we all suppose these are legally held (although decades ago, the Treasury thought otherwise, and for a time terrorized the hobby with the threat of seizing them).

Apart from the fact that it is impossible to effectively fight Uncle Sam, who has more money, attorneys, and tenacity than any collector will ever possess, it is my opinion that anyone owning a 1964-D Peace dollar or, for that matter, a 1974 aluminum cent, should be able to openly sell or display it. What do you think?

The "Thrill of the Chase" with Carson City Mint Coins

by Weimar W. White RCR 71 1988

The Carson City branch mint, under the superintendency of Abe Curry, opened its doors on January 6, 1870, but no coins were produced until February 11, 1870. The first coin struck was an 1870-CC silver dollar, of the Liberty Seated design.

There was much excitement in Carson City on that day, as the public welcomed the existence of the new, shiny cartwheels. The local newspaper made the following comment: "They are a sight for sore eyes, they have a most pleasant jingle, and they are worth eight cents more than two silver half dollars."

It was Nevada's most famous rich silver discovery, the Comstock Lode in 1859, just 14 to 15 miles away in the mining camps of Virginia City and Gold Hill, that prompted Congress to pass a bill (March 3, 1863) to establish a mint in the territory of Nevada.

Carson City was selected as the best location for the new mint because it was strategically located in relationship to the new mines, and there was a critical shortage of coins in the area.

Collectors have often wondered why so few Uncirculated Carson City minted coins exist for the first four years of its operations and why specimens seen are so well worn. The answer lies in the fact that there was an acute shortage of "real money" in the locality, and the few coins that were made were hastily spent. Carson City and Virginia City were in a rapid phase of building and expansion due to the wealth from the mines. Thus, the available money experienced a fast turnover. As a result, any Mint State example of a Carson City coin, made during the mint's first four years of existence, is a rare item today and is cherished by the fortunate owner.

The mint produced only silver and gold coins from 1870 to 1893, with three years of non-coinage activity (assay and refining operations) in between. As time passed, the rich silver-gold ore deposits became depleted, and the costs of the minting operations increased. Much pressure was exerted from Washington to close down the mint. A final blow was dealt when $75,549.75 in gold was found missing at the mint. The resulting scandal sealed the final doom of the Carson City Mint, and its doors were closed April 18, 1895.

Today the old mint is used for the Nevada State Museum, of which only a part is dedicated to exhibits relating to the past minting operations.

It is the romance of the "Old West," the discovery of silver and gold, the high-quality coinage produced at the mint, which excites the collector of Carson City coins. This excitement was further enhanced by the release of 2.9 million Uncirculated Carson City Morgan dollars to the public in the 1970s.

With this background about the mint, the author would like to share his thoughts concerning the availability of Carson City coins and ideas about collecting them.

It should be noted that the 56,660,299 coins (figures derived from *Guide Book*) struck at the mint (see Table I) are very low if compared to that of other U.S. mints.

The Carson City issues, including the major varieties that are collected, are as follows: 10 different dimes, two 20-cent pieces, nine quarters, 10 half dollars, four Liberty Seated dollars, 13 Morgan dollars, (the varieties of the 1879-CC and the 1880-CCs are not included in this tabulation), six trade dollars, and 19 each of the $5, $10, and $20 gold pieces. This comes to a total of 111 issues that can be collected. Few collectors have ever tried to assemble them all because of the great rarity of many of the coins.

However, one can avoid many of the frustrations experienced by the date collector by putting together a nice 10-piece Carson City type set. Such a set contains the seven types of silver coins as well as the $3 gold issues. The approximate cost for a matched set of the most "common" coins in Extremely Fine would be about $3,000. Such a set would certainly be regarded as very desirable and scarce. To assemble

The "Thrill of the Chase" with Carson City Mint Coins

an Uncirculated set, the present cost would be $9,000 and up. In the opinion of the author, only about 50 Mint State type sets are possible, due to the rarity of the Liberty Seated dollars.

Rarity Profile of Carson City Minted Coins

Because of the great collector interest in the coins produced by the Carson City mint, a general discussion about the major rarities in each series is given.

Dimes: The 1871-CC, 1872-CC, 1873-CC Without Arrows at the date (one Uncirculated specimen known, which is part of the Louis Eliasberg family collection), 1873-CC Arrows at Date and the 1874-CC are all major rarities in all grades. The 1875-CC above the bow mintmarked dime in Mint State can be purchased without much difficulty. On the other hand, the 1875-CC below the bow mint marked dime in Uncirculated condition is a Rarity-5 coin. The prices in *Guide Book* (1988) do not presently reflect the differences in rarity between these two coins. The most "common" Carson City dime in Uncirculated condition is the 1877-CC.

Twenty-cent pieces: Only the 1875-CC and the 1876-CC issues were produced. The author estimates that 400 to 1,200 examples of the 1875-CC issue exist in all states of preservation. It should be mentioned that it is extremely difficult to obtain an example of this date with the eagle's right wing and breast feathers strongly struck. The 1876-CC 20-cent piece is a well-known numismatic rarity, with most of the surviving examples (12 to 18) existing in Mint State. Genuine coins show doubling of the Liberty in the shield. Numismatists agree that virtually the entire mintage of this date was melted. Perhaps the few that were saved for assay purposes are the ones that survive today.

Quarters: The key coin in the series is the 1873-CC Without Arrows (three Mint State specimens are known). As with the 1873-CC No Arrows dime, most of the coins are believed to have been melted. This was because an increased legalized quantity of silver was added to certain 1873-CC coins, and the arrows at the date were added to signify the new weight. The rarest collectible date is the 1870-CC quarter, and specimens are difficult to obtain in any grade. Only the 1876-CC, 1877-CC and the 1878-CC quarters are fairly easy to locate in all grades. The rest of the dates are very scarce to rare. The 1877-CC is by far the most "common" Carson City quarter in Mint State.

Half dollars: The 1870-CC is regarded as the key coin in the series.

Randall Wiley has written an article in the *Gobrecht Journal*, Vol. 14, issue #40, estimating that only 120 to 150 coins now exist in all conditions, with over 70% of them being in grades of Fine or below. Only three of the specimens have any claim of being in Mint State condition. The 1871-CC, 1872-CC, 1873-CC With Arrows, 1873-CC Without Arrows, 1874-CC and the 1878-CC are all rarities in Uncirculated condition. The 1877-CC is the most "common" half dollar in Mint State.

Liberty Seated dollars: Just four dollars were made, which is only 0.03% of the total Carson City mintage. All Liberty Seated dollars are very rare in Mint State. The author estimates that about 27, 5, 16, and 3 specimens exist in Mint State for the 1870-CC, the 1871-CC, the 1872-CC and the 1873-CC, respectively. The four dollars as a group (about 50 known in Mint State) are more than 60,000 times rarer than Mint State Carson City Morgan dollars as a group. Present coin values of Liberty Seated dollars do not reflect the huge differences in rarity between the two types of dollars. In circulated grades, the 1871-CC and the 1873-CC issues are Rarity-5 coins. The 1872-CC dollar is slightly more available, giving it a rarity rating of Rarity-4. The 1870-CC dollar is a Rarity-3 coin, but it is difficult to locate in grades of Extremely Fine or better.

Morgan dollars: The 13 different Carson City dates are very popular with collectors, with the 1879-CC, the 1889-CC, and the 1893-CC being the key coins in the series. Even though many hundreds of Mint State 1889-CC dollars exist, they always command a high price when sold, because of a large collector/investor base for Morgan dollars. Two extremely difficult dates to find in MS-65 are the 1879-CC Capped Mintmark die variety (a minor variety) and the 1893-CC, both in deep prooflike condition. The author finds it interesting that the Capped Die variety (c/d) sells for less than the normal Carson City mintmarked coin when the former is much scarcer. Back in the 1960s, the author was instrumental in getting the (c/d) put into *Red Book* as a legitimate variety. The 1884-CC dollar is the most "common" of all the Carson City dates in Mint State.

Trade dollars: Of the six trade dollars, the 1878-CC and the 1873-CC are the rarest in Mint State. All Carson City Mint State examples, without chop marks, are very scarce to rare in this grade. It is difficult to estimate the number of Mint State specimens because of the number of "sliders" available, and since there is a tendency to overgrade these coins. With the exception of the 1878-CC trade dollar, most of the other dates are readily available in circulated grades.

Five-dollar gold: The first $5 gold pieces were struck on March 2, 1870, on the now-famous No. 1 coin press. In the author's opinion, Carson City $5 and $10 are presently vastly undervalued and unappreciated by the numismatic community. The mintages, in general, are very low, and most dates are rare! In the $5 series, the following dates are Rarity-5 or higher: 1870-CC, 1871-CC, 1872-CC, 1873-CC, 1874-CC, 1875-CC, 1876-CC, 1877-CC, 1878-CC, 1881-CC, 1883-CC, and the 1884-CC. All of these dates are rare in any state of preservation. The 1879-CC and the 1880-CC are very scarce in circulated grades and warrant a Rarity-4 rating. The 1882-CC, 1890-CC, 1891-CC, 1892-CC, and the 1893-CC are more "common" than the other issues mentioned, but they are still regarded as scarce. The 1891-CC in Mint State is by far the most "common" Carson City Mint State $5 gold piece. However, all gem Carson City Mint State $5 gold pieces are rare, in the author's opinion. In general, most Carson City Uncirculated gold coins are very "baggy" from being shipped to diverse locations in mint-sewn bags.

Ten-dollar gold: The first $10 gold eagles made their debut on February 14, 1870, and the local newspaper comment was that they were "beauties." During the 19 years of production, 299,778 coins were produced. This very small quantity of coins accounts for only 0.53% of the total Carson City mintage. The following dates are Rarity-5 or higher in all grades: 1870-CC, 1871-CC, 1872-CC, 1873-CC, 1874-CC, 1875-CC, 1876-CC, 1877-CC, 1878-CC, 1879-CC, and the 1882-CC. For these dates as a group, only a few Uncirculated examples are known. The 1880-CC, 1881-CC, 1883-CC, 1884-CC, and the 1893-CC are somewhat more available, but are still regarded as rare in any grade. The 1890-CC and the 1892-CC eagles are considered scarce dates, but do not have the same rarity status as the previous dates mentioned. The 1891-CC is the most "common" eagle, and it is relatively easy to obtain in all grades.

Twenty-dollar gold: Double eagles were the last of the three types of gold coins to be struck at the mint. It was not until the middle of March 1870 that the first coins containing almost a full troy ounce of gold rolled off the coin press. Tremendous pressure—up to 175 tons—was required to make a sharp impression on the round blanks of precious metal.

The 1870-CC is regarded as the rarest of the 19 Carson City double eagles issued. David Akers, in his book on double eagles, estimates that only 20 to 25 specimens are known in all grades. The average grade for this date is Very Fine, since virtually all of them went directly into circulation. Other rare dates in the series include the 1871-CC, 1891-CC, 1878-CC, 1879-CC, and the 1885-CC, listed in order of decreasing rarity. Many of the other issues are moderately rare to scarce. The four most "common" Uncirculated dates that can be purchased are the 1875-CC, 1880-CC, 1884-CC, and the 1893-CC.

Conclusion

It is hoped that the information contained in this article will give the reader a better understanding and appreciation of the coins manufactured by the Carson City Mint. The small number of coins minted and the fact that almost all of them, with the exception of Morgan dollars and some double eagles, went directly into circulation, resulting in Mint State examples of many issues being great rarities today.

The collecting of mintmarked coins only became popular at the turn of the century. The early collectors were generally content to purchase Proof coins, which they felt were superior in quality.

Whether the collector enjoys collecting Carson City coins by series or by type, the thrill of the "chase" is forever present. To own a part of the silver or gold mined from the Comstock Lode which is now in the form of an antique coin can be very satisfying.

There are many dates in the $5 and $10 gold series that are true rarities and which, at their present prices, are only a few times higher than the price of gold bullion. Opportunities for purchasing rare coins at bargain prices especially lie in these two Carson City series.

Lyman H. Low Tells His Story

by Lyman H. Low	1990

Introductory comments (by Q. David Bowers): In American numismatics in the late 19th and early 20th centuries Lyman Haines Low was a gigantic figure. A Bostonian by birth, he served in the Civil War, after which he did a stint as an intinerant salesman and, later, a part-time coin dealer, before deciding in 1883 to become a full-time professional numismatist. From that point onward, his contributions to the hobby were considerable.

Low's corpus of auction sales began with an auction dated Christmas Day, 1882, and continued through the J.C. Hills Collection sale held in two parts, the second on April 4-5, 1924. John W. Adams, in *United States Numismatic Literature, Volume One* (Mission Viejo, CA: George Frederick Kolbe Publications, 1982), pays the following tribute:

"Low never handled the largest collections, nor did he do a big business overall. However, for 18 years (1891-1907) he served as co-editor of the prestigious *American Journal of Numismatics*; he wrote a landmark monograph on Hard Times tokens; and he singlehandledly compiled [coin value guides for Scott]. Despite such prodigious output, Low's best performances, in our opinion, may be found in his auction catalogues. These are characterized by painstaking descriptions, exceptionally conservative grading, and a wealth of background commentary... A complete set of his 212 sales would contain more information to be found nowhere else than any other body of literature that comes to mind.

The Numismatist's Topside Companion

"Lyman Low catalogues are virtually unknown in U.S. numismatics today; however, it seems safe to predict that the man will inevitably be 'discovered, and his catalogues will take their rightful place among the classics of our hobby."

It is not that Low himself is completely unknown, for today we still attribute Hard Times tokens to the 183 numbers assigned by Low at the turn of the century. When Russell Rulau vastly expanded and updated Low's work in 1980, he paid Low the tribute of assigning new "Low numbers" to hundreds of additional pieces.

At 10:30 a.m., Monday, September 28, 1908, the convention of the American Numismatic Association opened in Philadelphia, with President Farran Zerbe officiating. A hearty welcome on behalf of local collectors and professionals was extended by Henry Chapman. A few hours later, in the afternoon, Lyman H. Low addressed the assembled conventioneers. By that time Low was at the peak of his profession and was widely respected not only as a numismatic auctioneer but also as a dedicated scholar and a generally "nice fellow." Low told the audience how he began his profession, and gave advice to coin buyers. His comments were reprinted in the October 1908 issue of *Mehl's Numismatic Monthly*, and for the possible interest of the present audience they are given here:

Lyman Low's Own Story

I propose to occupy a few moments of your time with some personal reminiscences and a few suggestions, in the hope that they may prove, if not entertaining, possibly of some benefit. But I must first express my great gratification at meeting so many who have been interested in matters which have concerned the greater part of my life. My pleasure in this direction has heretofore been limited to the occasional visits of friends to my place of business, and the meetings at coin sales. Today so many familiar faces greet me that I am almost overwhelmed; my cup is full.

Coins first attracted my attention in 1856. The fever continued possibly for a year, and then other subjects engrossed me, doubtless from lack of congenial companionship, for I knew but one collector, and it was he who inspired me. I had not then learned of a dealer, though Henry Cook of Boston—my native place—was engaged in the business at that time. The summit of joy was reached and my El Dorado found at the tollhouse on the Boston side of Chelsea Ferry, where I made weekly visits on Saturday afternoons and looked over a box of odd pieces. It was the custom of the tollman to accept anything having the semblance of a coin. If it proved to be something else than a piece of U.S. mintage it was thrown into this box. But nothing of special importance was ever secured, for my knowledge was limited and pocketbook small. My recollections are that Connecticut cents, Hard Times tokens, and an occasional storecard composed the bulk of my treasures. It seems worthy of comment that I never found a half cent in any of the claims I prospected. I was certain at that period none was in circulation in Massachusetts. When the Civil War came on I took my collection to a State Street broker, and sold it for $5. I have never forgotten my first small accumulation.

During the war more important matters demanded my time, and in the years which followed until 1878 the subject was dormant. In that year, when a commercial traveler, I was sojourning in the West, just below St. Paul. Many foreign copper and silver coins were in circulation in that community, and I soon found myself making a collection of the various kinds I met with. By this means I became acquainted with three collectors in the town, and their hoards were sufficient to rekindle the flame of 20 years previous. My ardor was thoroughly aroused, and the interest I took was intense. I dreamed and talked of coins incessantly, but I soon became rational and launched into the subject in sober earnest. Almost immediately I began to sell as well as purchase. The captures, whether of pieces or of customers, were not large or important. In the fall of 1879, after returning to New York from one of my trips, I passed the old store of Bangs & Co., on Broadway, opposite Astor Place, and read the bulletin at the door, "Coin Sale Today." A few brisk steps took me up to those long, flannel-covered tables, which some of you perhaps remember. I attended the sale that afternoon, and most of those that followed, whenever I was able to do so.

In 1883 I made the dealing in coins my exclusive business, beginning at 838 Broadway. When I offered my collection, numbering some 15,000 pieces, to buyers, it was chiefly composed of copper coins. My career since that time is fairly recorded in the catalogues of my public sales, the first being that of the late Alexander Balmanno of Brooklyn. So much for my early reminiscences; of later days I need not enlarge in this company.

The Association, whose representatives are here assembled in such goodly numbers, from widely distant points, has been the means of drawing together a large body of collectors, and uniting in its membership those of kindred tastes, and its good results are apparent on every side. No other plan could have succeeded so well. It has raised the standard of the science, has developed interest, diffused a large amount of information, and has greatly augmented the ranks of coin-lovers and students. Too great commendation cannot be bestowed on the memory and labors of the late Dr. Heath, whom we justly regard as the founder of the Association, its father, its faithful guide until the close of his career. He was eminently fitted to undertake the work of its establishment—exceptionally so, indeed—and I do not know of another who could have accomplished so much. I hope our future may be guided with equal zeal, wisdom, earnestness, and success, under the leadership of men whose aims may be fairly compared with the high ideals which constantly actuated our lamented friend, who from the first stood so firmly and so justly at the helm.

Among those who are still with us, and whose works are beyond praise, Farran Zerbe and Howland Wood are names that I am sure deserve the special commendation of every member for what they have accomplished for our Association by their able efforts and untiring industry.

There are others whom it would be fitting to mention, who have contributed to our success, but the list would be long, and they are so well known to you, it is needless for me to name them at this time. It would be a pleasure in this connection to recall also some of the prominent collectors and dealers who have gone before us—Cogan, and Strobridge, and Woodward, Stickney and Smith, and many more—but I must content myself with the observation that their memory is still respected and revered. Their work and the inspiration of their example have set a standard to which we may well aspire.

There are many subjects that are proper to bring to your notice, as collectors of coins and members of this grand Association. It cannot be expected that all of them will be embodied in any single address, and possibly of all that should be some must necessarily be omitted.

On the commercial side there should be cultivated reasonableness and all the tendencies that lead up to it. From the expert may justly be expected intelligence in the matter of attribution, a thorough knowledge of varieties and values, accurate and impartial descriptions of ratings of prices, and reliable judgment as to their genuineness. There are honest and intelligent differences of opinion, which will occasionally arise, and it is here that both sides should be willing to meet each other with a sincere desire to accomplish a fair adjustment; each should endeavor to be magnanimous, and positively and finally discharge the matter without seeking to be merely the victor.

The buyer who gives an unlimited bid for a lot in an auction sale runs a dangerous risk of disappointment. It is equally a mistake to instruct your commissioner to use his judgment, unless some intimation of value is communicated. Purchases made under such conditions too often result in dissatisfaction, and sometimes in unpleasant feeling—the view of the buyer and his agent not concurring. The better way is first to obtain an opinion as to what the lot or piece, in the judgment of the dealer, may sell for, and then make a definite offer for it and stand by the result. Again, too much care cannot be given to preparing bids for a sale. Make your figures plain and unmistakable, and be sure that the lot numbers are the ones you desire to bid on. Much confusion follows errors in this direction, and they are very difficult to adjust. The matter concerns not only the buyer, but the owner who has been informed of the results, as well as the expert and those who have made unsuccessful bids, which would perhaps have secured the lot but for the error.

A word on books of reference. Much satisfaction and success are obtained by the collector who forms a library and reads it. What others have learned by their studies, recorded and put in print, particularly those who have treated some special series, is at his command, and is of value to him. One may intelligently collect by such a guide, besides saving a great deal of time. He who reads with care certainly has the advantage over those who do not have, or fail to consult, text books. It is not too much to say that every branch of the science has been reviewed, and in some instances by many authors. With very few exceptions the most modern compilations are considered the best. They generally gather the good results obtained by their predecessors, eliminate or expose their errors, and record the new theories with additional facts which have been carefully worked out. It is, however, the pioneer who furnishes the foundation, besides giving information that might be very difficult for later students to obtain. New and old authorities should be sought for and searched by students, and what one author has omitted may be of special interest to others.

The field for collecting is very large, and indeed practically unlimited. It is often the case that a beginner seize everything, particularly if the "attack" upon him is severe. It is more than likely, as time goes on, that he will settle upon some branch that has proved specially attractive to him, and then his best efforts will be developed. Collectors like these furnish welcome contributions to the literature on our favorite science. Many dark ways have thus been illuminated and mysteries solved.

On counterfeiting and impositions. The incentive to imitate rare pieces has always been present, and in the United States series the field has been very large. From 1793 to 1856 every variety of note has its imitations. Electrotypes, when artistically made, are the most apt to pass without suspicion, but the sealing of two parts together—for the obverse and reverse must of course be produced separately—will reveal their falsity. Those not so skillfully made may have very good surfaces, but the edges will be found to have fine lines, the mark of a file running around the circle, not crosswise.

The most dangerous imposition is made by the mating or muling process of two pieces. The obverse or reverse is bored out or cut to the edge, in cup form, and into this one side of another coin is fitted. The border line or circle hides the insertion, and thus the original edge—usually a guide in detecting frauds—remains intact.

Casts are the most easily detected. They simply require close inspection, when the coarseness of the surface will be observed. They are frequently tooled, but such attempts to improve seldom deceive a careful eye. False pieces are occasionally holed and so defaced that their condition may further parry suspicion. Amusement is now and then the parent of counterfeits, especially electrotypes, but downright fraud, with the intention and hope of gain, is the incentive in most cases.

Finally, the counterfeits of colonial pieces struck from dies made by J.A. Bolen and the half cents of 1796, executed under the direction of Dr. Edwards, are not easily distinguished from genuine pieces, inasmuch as the workmanship is excellent; they are splendid imitations, and of a very different style of execution from those previously mentioned. Much more might be said on this subject, but it is of sufficient importance to be discussed in a carefully prepared paper or address. It is a good rule not to accept as genuine any piece which meets with your disfavor upon first sight. However slight your suspicions are, I assume they will never be disproved or removed.

Lyman H. Low Tells His Story

A hint upon the use of the magnifying glass. The natural eye in its youth and perfection is unequal to the critical examination of pieces, in the search for varieties and peculiarities in dies and for the detection of alterations and forgeries. Accustom yourselves to this helper, which leads to ease, comfort, and knowledge.

In the matter of ephemeral issues, especially, too little is thought of the events which evoked them. While we are in a position to obtain facts in detail, we should secure and record them. They may later prove of vital interest—if not to us, to some future collector. How much value a knowledge of the occasion of some of these pieces would give to local history, no one knows better than he whose search for information has been baffled, in spite of his most strenuous efforts, but which some careful collector might have permanently recorded when the piece appeared. We may laugh at the obsequious adulation of Boswell, but without his record of what others thought trifles how little should we know of the private life of his ponderous idol, the famous philosopher, Dr. Samuel Johnson!

Editor's note: Thanks to Dr. Joel Orosz and Remy Bourne for calling our attention to this and other early items from Mehl's Numismatic Monthly.

Supergrade Coins

by Scott A. Travers RCR 90 1992

Recently in the Rare Coin Review *your editor, quoting Maurice Rosen, suggested that certain coins in very high grades were overpriced. Scott Travers took exception to this view, and we invited him to contribute the following article.*

Car buyers don't usually think of a Rolls-Royce or Mercedes-Benz as a bargain. And well-to-do car buyers—tend not to talk about such trivial matters as price. It's considered poor form: Anyone who can afford this kind of car isn't supposed to worry about the cost. Still, there's nothing wrong with driving—and getting—a bargain, even if the money you save by doing so is frosting on the cake, rather than basic meat and potatoes on the table.

I don't claim to be an expert on the car market, but I do know that luxury *coins*—those we call "supergrade" coins—are very attractively priced right now. Indeed, there are many that qualify as bargains, based on their current price levels compared with those of commoner and not-so-costly coins.

Some of these coins are priced beyond the budgets of ordinary hobbyists. However, many others are surprisingly affordable—and they have enormous potential to rise in value sharply when the next big market upturn takes place. It is generally accepted that "supergrade" coins are those that merit a grade of at least MS-66, or Proof-66, on the 1-to-70 grading scale employed in the marketplace today. Some would limit the term to coins in grades no lower than 67; still others would restrict it to coins graded at least 68. But, for the purposes of this article, supergrade coins are those that have been certified in grades that range from 66 to 70.

Grab your attention

With few exceptions, supergrade coins, like most U.S. coins, have declined in value during the last several years. Most of them are priced today much lower than they were worth at the last big market peak in the late spring of 1989. This is hardly news. What *should* raise your eyebrows, though, and grab your immediate attention, is the fact that in many instances, supergrade coins have suffered a greater loss in value—proportionately speaking, that is—than coins in lesser grades that are far more common.

Common sense tells us that this is illogical: Supergrade coins possess quality, beauty and rarity in much greater abundance than their cousins farther down the grading scale. Their flawless surfaces and radiant lustre give them tremendous eye appeal—and even in cases where a coin's total mintage is relatively high, few examples may survive (or may have been made to begin with) in levels of preservation this magnificent.

Supergrade coins are still much higher-priced than lower-tier coins in the Mint State and Proof grading range. There are many instances, though, where the differential today is significantly smaller than it was at the market peak in 1989. The overall market slump has substantially lowered the ratio by which the prices of many supergrade coins exceed those of lesser coins in the same denomination and series.

Consider what we've witnessed with Barber half dollars in Proof. On June 2, 1989, a popular pricing guide for certified coins listed a value of $27,000 for type coin Barber halves graded Proof-67 by the Professional Coin Grading Service (PCGS) and $6,775 for specimens graded Proof-65. In short, a Proof-67 piece was worth about four times more than a Proof-65.

On June 12, 1992, the comparable price-guide values were $7,900 in Proof-67 and $3,400 in Proof-65—a ratio of just 2.3 to 1. After three years of generally downward movement in the marketplace, Proof-67 coins in this particular series were worth only slightly more than twice as much as Proof-65s. The price ratio had been cut nearly in half. (NOTE: These listings were for sight-unseen coins. Naturally, coins with unusual aesthetic appeal wholesale for *considerably* more.)

Mint-State 20-cent pieces illustrate the same peculiar phenomenon.

Ratio of 4 to 1

On June 2, 1989, the listed prices for type-coin 20-cent pieces graded by the Numismatic Guaranty Corporation of America (NGC) were $96,500 in MS-67 and $14,500 in MS-65. Thus, a 20-cent piece graded MS-67 was worth about 6.7 times as much as its counterpart in MS-65. On June 12, 1992, the values were $25,500 in MS-67 and $6,200 in MS-65—a ratio of only slightly more than 4 to 1.

Proof trade dollars provide yet another example of coins whose value has declined proportionately more in supergrade levels than in slightly lower grades. In June 1989, Proof-67 trade dollars were roughly 4.5 times more expensive than Proof-65 specimens. In June 1992, that ratio had shrunk to only about 3 to 1.

Less desirable today?

Are Proof Barber halves, MS-67 20-cent pieces and Proof-67 Trade dollars that much less desirable today? Certainly not. But the market for big-ticket coins is relatively thin, and it's my judgment that bigger-budget buyers went to the sidelines in proportionately greater numbers during the slump. Once the market rebounds, as it inevitably will, and once the recession eases its grip on the overall economy, big buyers and big money will resume their pursuit of rare coins, and supergrade coins will be primary targets for acquisition.

A few skeptics have argued unpersuasively that supergrade coins are overrated—that they never were really worth the premiums people were paying and thus were due for a fall. Having observed the marketplace closely throughout its years of greatest growth and greatest volatility, I can assure you that this is a serious misconception. If anything, supergrade coins are *scarcer* than previously thought, especially in the very highest grades.

It may well be that the misconception stems from the fact that we have seen a series of spectacular coins appear on the market in recent months. This may have led to the totally false conclusion that these coins represented the tip of the iceberg—that many more are stashed away and waiting to be released at an opportune time.

It's true that there have been unusually large numbers of "wonder coins" in evidence of late. But I consider this a matter of serendipity—simply a happy coincidence, if you will. Just as we were treated to a series of landmark auctions in the early 1980s, when the Garrett, Eliasberg and Brand coins came up for sale in quick succession at memorable auctions conducted by Bowers and Ruddy, so, too, we have been blessed by successive private sales of sensational supergrade coins in the recent past.

Nearly perfect Proof sets

It was my privilege to participate in the dispersal of some of these coins. Early in 1992, the numismatic world was amazed by the appearance of a group of 25 nearly perfect Proof sets covering the period from 1892 to 1916. These sets had been assembled by John Story Jenks, a much-admired numismatist of the late 19th and early 20th centuries. Dozens of the coins trembled on the threshold of perfection. Six of them, in fact, were certified as Proof-69 by NGC—a company that had given that grade to only one other coin in nearly five years of operation. I take great pride in the fact that I acquired four of those six coins for fortunate clients. Neither I nor my clients had ever beheld coins of such incredible perfection—and it's possible we may never see any that surpass them, no matter how long and hard we search in years to come.

Years from now, with the benefit of hindsight, we may very well conclude that supergrade coins were underrated and underpriced even at the market highs of 1989. I am firmly convinced that when the market turnaround occurs, these coins will soar in value faster and farther than any other segment of the marketplace.

They're even better buys—even bigger bargains—today than they were in 1989. So if you have room in your numismatic "garage" for a Rolls or a Mercedes, now is the time to hurry down to your favorite "luxury coin" dealer and take a test-drive.

Think how proud you'll be to own such beautiful coins. And don't be ashamed to think—and even talk—about the savings.

Five tips on buying supergrade coins

(1) Buy only coins that are truly rare. Just because a coin is in a high level of preservation, that in itself doesn't necessarily mean the coin is rare. Put another way, a coin can be supergrade without being super-rare. Conversely, other types of coins can be downright rare in less-than-supergrade condition—sometimes even in higher-level circulated grades. An MS-67 Liberty Head double eagle, or $20 gold piece, isn't truly rare, for example. It's certainly desirable, but quite a few

"Lib" twenties exist in the supergrade range. I'm not saying that you should never buy one, only that you should be cognizant of these coins' relative availability and not pay a price that is inappropriately high.

Late-date Proofs are exceptionally common in the supergrade range, even in grades as high as Proof-68 and 69. For that reason, you should steer clear of dealers who present—and price—these coins as if they were scarce or rare. Proof examples of recent U.S. commemorative coins fall into this category, right along with regular-issue Proofs. Some of these are even quite plentiful with grading-service certification as Proof-70!

Incidentally, you won't find any late-date Proofs in holders from the Numismatic Guaranty Corporation of America (NGC). For several years, NGC has made it a policy not to accept such coins for certification—simply because they *are* so common and some unscrupulous dealers have been using the certification of these coins (by companies other than NGC) as a marketing device to overcharge unwary customers.

(2) Deal only with reputable dealers—dealers you've done business with before, whose reputations are important to them and whom you know you can trust.

All this may seem obvious, but a lot of people forget it in the excitement of seeing and desiring a coin that really appeals to them. Often, the value of a supergrade coin may fall within a gray area; there may not have been enough recorded sales of similar pristine material to establish a firm price level. In such cases, you as the buyer are more dependent than usual on the seller's forthrightness and integrity. If you're doing business with a reputable dealer who prizes his reputation, he'll be sure to work with you and help you understand the coin's true value.

(3) In checking current values for supergrade coins, consult the Certified Coin Exchange and other price guides which are reasonably accurate for grade levels up to Mint State and Proof-67.

The Certified Coin Exchange (or CCE) is actually very accurate even for coins graded as high as MS- and Proof-68. I have acquired a number of coins graded 68, and have found CCE to be a good barometer of the market. As a rule, I purchase such coins for very slight advances over CCE's MS or Proof-68 prices for the given coins, then sell them to my clients at specified commissions—with all these amounts being fully disclosed.

(4) Examine each coin carefully to satisfy yourself that it's chemically stable and thus will not deteriorate, and check it regularly after you purchase it.

In order to merit a grade of 68 or 69, a coin must have virtual perfection—almost no perceptible flaw. If that coin subsequently suffers even the slightest damage or deterioration, its value can decline by tens of thousands of dollars. With that in mind, you owe it to yourself—not to mention future generations of collectors—to do everything possible to keep each dazzling supergrade coin pristine and problem-free. If you detect even the most subtle evidence of potential trouble, you should have the coin removed from its holder and chemically neutralized with trichlorofluoroethane. This is a harmless, highly evaporative form of freon which will safeguard the coin's surface.

(5) Don't put all your eggs in one basket. Diversification is desirable in any form of collecting, and this applies to supergrade coins as much as it does to others. Don't buy only coins in the supergrade range; buy other kinds, as well—coins of different grades, and coins of different types.

This will not only broaden your horizons as a hobbyist but also spread your risk as an investor, even if you don't really think of yourself as such.

To Err is Human (and Can be Funny)

by Q. David Bowers   1993

The following was written for "The Joys of Collecting" column in COIN WORLD, *1993.*

Recently, *Coin World* reader Melvin Hazard penned this letter to me: "I feel that Mr. Madison deserves the greatest commemorative coin ever. According to your February 8th column, Madison died on March 6, 1812, and continued serving as president until March 4, 1817. That is some feat!"

Aha! A typographical error, and probably one made by the *Coin World* graphics crew, I thought to myself. Alas, upon checking my original manuscript, I found that *I* was the culprit. For the record, Madison died on June 28, 1836. Thus, he was not dead during his presidency—although it may not be beyond the realm of possibility for this to have been the case, especially as viewed by his political opposition.

This set me to thinking about other typographical goofs. Over the years, I have enjoyed "collecting" errors as I have seen them in print, much as Richard Lederer and Jay Leno have collected mistakes and double-entendre newspaper headlines (and have published books about them).

Here are some I have found (these were not my errors, by the way, but I have made my share):

▼ 1864 two-cent piece with IN GOLD WE TRUST motto in small letters (there are those who do, indeed, place their faith in yellow metal).

The Numismatist's Topside Companion

▼ 1926-S Oregon Trial half dollar. (There are legal proceedings in Oregon, I am sure, but I didn't know that they were worth commemorating on a coin.)

▼ 1795 silver dollar "hold at the top." (Probably, the coin was *holed* at the top, for we all know that it should be held by the *edge*.)

▼ 1964 Poof set (a group of coins used for a Hallowe'en trick?).

▼ The Federal Reverse System (I guess the government indeed goes backwards on occasion).

▼ 1842 Proof half cent with small zerries on the reverse (What are these? Leprechauns?).

▼ 1836 Gold Brick dollar (a Gobrecht dollar used in a con scheme?).

▼ 1936 Cincinnati commemorative half dollar with portrait of "Stephen Faster" on the obverse. (Is Stephen Faster like Speedy Gonzales?)

▼ "Cannons" of the Rare Coin Dealers Association, RCDA. (I presume that *canons,* or a listing of ethical rules, was intended, but perhaps the RCDA had some "big shots"; this was used in a full-page ad.)

▼ 1955 Double Dye cent (perhaps it was "dyed" or recolored, even twice!).

▼ 1907 Cornet $10 gold piece (was Miss Liberty playing a trumpet?). Such things make numismatics a lot of fun!

Two (Numismatic) Resolutions for a Happy New Year

by Q. David Bowers   1993

The following was written for "The Joys of Collecting" column in COIN WORLD, *1993.*

It's 1993, and a dandy time to make some numismatic resolutions for the New Year. This week I'll give as a starter two ideas guaranteed to increase your enjoyment and knowledge, and at very little expense.

1. Pick out three or four scarce coins of interest. They do not have to be in a series you collect. In fact, if they are in some other series, all the better. Select something that is not extremely rare, yet not extremely common—the type of coin that trades regularly throughout the year, but not in quantity. Suggestions include items like an 1857 half cent, 1823 large cent, 1877 Indian cent, 1844 Liberty Seated silver dollar, or a date of Charlotte or Dahlonega gold coin.

Get a pad of lined yellow paper and as many past issues of *Coin World* as you can find, plus whatever you can track down in the way of auction catalogues (with prices realized), numismatic periodicals, and the like. Make a listing of how many times the coins you selected have appeared on the market in the past year. When you are finished you will have a complete understanding of a coin with which you may not have been familiar earlier.

This idea came from a member of our staff who, several years ago, had recently joined our organization, and who was confused at first with the more than 100 varieties of Morgan silver dollars, different pricing structures, and a wide array of grades. She decided to pick an 1885-CC Morgan dollar and study it all by itself. A couple hours later, the 1885-CC made a lot of sense—she realized that most specimens offered were in Mint State, that worn examples were very rare, that prices varied, that some advertisers were specific as to what they offered (such as MS-63 PCGS) and others gave vague descriptions ("selected beautiful example," etc.) and so on. From that point it was a simple step to understand other Morgan dollars. Now, she is very conversant with the series. Who knows, this suggestion may launch you into a new collecting area!

2. The second resolution: Take $100 and buy that amount worth of interesting numismatic books. Dr. William H. Sheldon's *Penny Whimsy* is a great start. In a recent letter, Dr. Harry E. Salyards stated that one reason the collecting of early cents 1793-1814 was so popular today is that collectors had the Sheldon book as a guide and inspiration. Even if you do not contemplate collecting large cents, there is a tremendous amount of fascinating information in the book about Mint procedures, grading, and the like. Also buy a copy of Don Taxay's *U.S. Mint and Coinage*. I absolutely and positively guarantee that if you read this book from cover to cover you will vastly expand your appreciation of United States coins of all kinds, and will be one of the most knowledgeable individuals in your circle of numismatic friends. With the money left, pick out a few other interesting titles.

Researching the 1894-S Dime

by James G. (Jim) Johnson, N.L.G.   RCR 64 1987

James G. (Jim) Johnson wrote, for many years, the "Fair to Very Fine" column for Coin World. *The 1894-S dime is, of course, one of America's most famous rarities.*

The auction of an 1894-S dime at the September 25-26 convention of the Northern California Numismatic Association brings back interesting and personal memories of the first published pedigree of that and the other known specimens of the coin, as well as just how many are known.

Back about 1971 or 1972, I acquired one of these coins, a well-circulated piece, and tried to find out more about it. Not much was known. An auction description by Stack's (1957) said "seven or eight are known." New Netherlands (1958), "Possibly seven examples known to us." Hydeman Sale (1961), "There seem to be only seven known specimens."

At the Northern California Numismatic Association auction, the description stated that 12 are known. An official of the A.N.A. a few years ago said 14 were known. Both are right and both are wrong. To state it briefly, there are 10 known authenticated pieces and that's it. The other four either have never been authenticated by any accepted authority as genuine or in the case of two, are believed by some to be fakes. One of them was owned by Abe Kosoff who wrote to tell me he had destroyed it.

That information was published by me in "Collectors' Clearinghouse" of *Coin World,* in the September 13, 1972 issue and supplemented in the same place, June 27, 1973, for the first time. With some minor differences. Walter Breen backed me up in his *Encyclopedia of United States...Proof Coins* in 1977. He changed the order but essentially his list was identical to mine, including the total of authenticated pieces. He added a couple more I didn't know about.

I retract that. He had nine authenticated pieces to my 10, but the one we differed on was authenticated by Stuart Mosher of New Netherlands and checked by Stack's twice which, for my money, makes it genuine.

Why this emphasis on "authenticated" pieces I'm not sure. It is taken as a matter of fact that counterfeits of ordinary coins are both illegal and unwanted in collections or for spending. Altered collector coins are usually considered the same way. Rarities seem to be on a different level, but I don't know why. To me, a fake is a fake—rarity or not—and I don't want it.

Getting back to the subject of this article—the research—I first tried to find out what had been printed about the 1894-S dime, a coin that Breen calls "the most mysterious of San Francisco mintages."

The earliest known published reference was in *The Numismatist* for June, 1900, in which Editor George Heath quotes the mint as saying, "Of the 24 struck, 14 went into circulation, the other 10 being restruck," meaning melted down and used in other coinage. There is no statement about why they were struck.

In 1928, Heath quoted Farran Zerbe as saying that in 1905, the Mint told him that $2.40 was needed to balance Mint accounts at the end of the fiscal year (June 30, 1894) so they struck 24 dimes of which all but two or three went into circulation. Heath said also that in 1928 the whereabouts of only four specimens were known.

Keep in mind that Mint statements are official and reflect what is supposed to have been done in any given case. They do not reflect what actually was done in any given case. We at *Coin World* learned that lesson from experience after many years of dealing with the Mint. So those two somewhat conflicting Mint statements reflect only what was the official story at that time.

No other general statements about the 1894-S dime appeared in print until my 1973 story was published. Then I got a letter from Guy L. Chapman of California. He wrote that in 1954, Earl Parker showed him two of the coins. Parker had just acquired them from Hallie Daggett, daughter of the 1894 Mint Superintendent.

She told him this:

(Briefly stated since the story has been quoted many times since I printed it.) Her father was asked by some banker friends to strike some dimes for them. He had 24 struck and gave three to each of seven people, and the other three to his daughter. She spent one and sold the other two to Parker in 1954.

Although quoted widely, Walter Breen and Dave Bowers are about the only ones who gave me credit for first printing it. There is no good reason to doubt its truthfulness as Hallie Daggett was present in 1894, which also implies some thing special about the occasion. Mint superintendents' young daughters aren't usually around when Mint operations are carried out. Maybe it was Sunday Anyway, in 1954 she had the dimes!

This story also could easily explain why most of the known specimens are in "Mint" condition. Those people who got them from Daggett didn't get them to spend! And most of our pedigrees probably date back to those who acquired them from the original owners, although they probably did not publish the fact, for fairly obvious reasons. The original owners didn't want it known where they got them.

So much for original history of the 1894-S dimes. I don't expect any more facts will be known until the Mint releases the San Francisco Mint records now in dead storage in San Mateo, California, or so Breen told me. No reason has so far been given for keeping them in secrecy. Somebody might well use the Freedom of Information Act to get them out. I have never had time or the initiative to do it!

Something more has been discovered about the presently-known specimens. From an authority who has examined five of them, we have a statement that two obverse dies and one reverse were used to strike those pieces.

How many dies were sent to San Francisco and how many were actually used is buried in the storage files in San Mateo. Also buried there is the manner of striking, whether or not all or any were intentionally made as Proofs or whether they were what are frequently called "new die" Proofs. Some dealers have described some of the known specimens as *Proofs,* some have called them "Uncirculated," and others have not said. We don't know what Daggett said, as his official report is also in San Mateo.

Breen wrote me back then that he agreed with the *Coin World* definition of Proofs that the manner of striking and preparation of dies and planchets were what made Proofs, and that only the San Mateo records could tell. He did say that the five he examined were of such high quality that they were evidently special in some way, but whether they were given several blows in an old screw press as Proofs were made then, he couldn't tell.

In his 1977 book, he does list them under branch mint Proofs, so he either changed his mind or did it for special reasons. On the other hand, Wayte Raymond omits them from his list of branch mint Proofs. So you take your choice.

That is one argument we won't get into, as to whether those coins are Proofs or business strikes. Too many authorities disagree on definitions. To some, if a coin looks like a Proof, it is one. To others, the manner of striking is the significant factor as well as proper preparation of both dies and planchets.

I mention this in passing: These pieces could well have been struck individually in any manner desired, on any handy press. Some may have been given "special attention," some may not have.

The dies had to have been new, and if the pressman took time to switch obverse dies in making only 24 coins, he wasn't striking them in any hurry. "New die" Proofs are the first few coins struck off new dies before the polish has worn off. The pressman could well have switched obverse dies just for that reason, to make them all look like Proofs! Or, contrary to Hallie Daggett's recollection, the coins could have been struck at more than one occasion.

In doing my basic research on these coins, I queried every major dealer in the country, who was known to have either handled one of them or who might have, since about 1940. All were cooperative and contributed what they knew or substantiated what others said. Then I correlated the different letters to eliminate duplication of reports, that is, when two dealers obviously discussed the same coin. Most of the letters were pretty specific as to dates of handling, where they got the coins and in most cases who they sold them to.

Over 1972 and 1973, I reached the total of 10 authenticated specimens, of which two were well circulated. In the 1972 story, I also mentioned two known fakes, but *Coin World* policy prevented me from being more specific than that. Breen lists my 10 and two more, i.e., 12, but says three of them have never been authenticated, so we didn't differ that much, and I disagree with one of those three, which gets back to my 10 known genuine pieces.

Two other lists have been published, one by Robert L. Hughes in 1979, and one by Bill Gibbs in *Coin World* in 1984. All four lists use my original list but change the order and the piece numbers. Gibbs uses Breen's numbers and order of the pieces. None of them gives me credit for listing them first. Hughes and Gibbs add a few later transactions I would not have known about in 1972, because they had not yet happened.

Breen used two words in connection with some of his listed pieces, "unseen" and "unverified." From the context, I interpret those words to mean, in the first case, that he accepted authenticity without personally seeing the coin, and in the second case that the coin had never been authenticated by anybody he accepted as an authority.

The one piece we differed on was my CC-10, which I will now call J-10. It is also B(reen)-12 and H(ughes)-9. This is the well-circulated piece known as Romito-Monesano. Breen called it "unverified." Romito acquired it in 1911 when there weren't many fakes running around, Stuart Mosher of New Netherlands pronounced it genuine, and Stack's accepted it for auction twice, and they were fussy.

So, for my money, by 1973 there were 10 authenticated and genuine specimens, and still are in 1986. There may be 11, based on circumstantial evidence. B-8 is the piece in the Hartford, Connecticut State Library which is presumed to be the same piece mentioned in the 1900 *The Numismatist* as having been found in San Francisco by J.C. Mitchelson. He bequeathed his collection to that Library, according to Breen. I suggest it may be genuine simply because in 1900 who knew enough about 1894-S dimes to fake one? No one has ever intimated that the coin is other than an authentic example.

So we won't know for sure if there are 11 until somebody checks out that Hartford specimen, but I suspect that there are 11. Every time an 1894-S dime has come on the public market without a pedigree, I have written the dealer involved to ask the source of the coin and which of the 10 known listed specimens it was. In that way I have pretty much kept track of where the coins are. I still have no reason to change my original listing.

Followed by some further comments, I now give my original list, augmented by later transactions, with cross reference to Hughes and Breen numbers, for those who are familiar with them.

J-1, B-9, H-6: Rappaport (where did he get it?), Kagin's, Reuther, Kreisberg, Bowers, Eastern estate.

J-2, B-1, H-7: Newcomer (where did he get it?), Boyd, Kosoff, Neil, Mehl, Hydeman, Kosoff, Bowers-Empire, Hazen Hinman, Jim Kelly, Young, RARCOA, Gillio, in the 1986 N.C.N.A. sale.

J-3, B-2, H-5: Clapp, Stack's, Eliasberg.

J-4, B-7, H-4: Cass, Stack's, Bowers, Norweb.

J-5, B-5, H-8: Daggen, Parker, Dan Brown, Stack's, a Chicago collector.

J-6, B-3, H-3: Clapp, Eliasberg, Lee, Stack's, a New York collector.

J-7, B-11, H-10: (well-circulated) Friedberg-Gimbels, Kagin's, New Netherlands, Kagin's, Harmer-Rooke, Jim Johnson (the writer of this article), Old Roman, Hughes, an Eastern collector, Hughes (offered for sale in 1979 when his listing was published).

J-8, B-4, H-2: Stack's, James A. Stack estate (no relation to the dealer).

J-9, B-6, H-1: Daggett, Parker, W.R. Johnson, Kreisberg, World-Wide, Bowers, a Midwestern collector.

J-10, B-12, H-9: (well-circulated) Romito (acquired in 1911), Montesano, an Eastern dealer, Hughes, an Eastern collector. (Breen calls it "unverified" but for reasons given above, I disagree with him.)

That is my original listing in the order I published it, and as printed but renumbered by both Breen and Hughes. Also added are later transactions as recorded by Bill Gibbs who used Breen's numbering and order.

But, and it's a big BUT, Breen had two more numbers and an unnumbered specimen. Here they are. (Hughes omitted all three.)

B-8: Mitchelson, Connecticut State Library in Hartford. (As mentioned above, this is probably the same piece mentioned in the 1900 *The Numismatist*. Breen calls it "unverified" and it probably is that, but for reasons given I feel it is genuine.)

B-10: (Circulated-EF) California collector, Kagin's, another collector, Kagin's, National Coin Company, Superior, Jerry Buss, Superior, Michelle Johnson. (Breen also calls this "unverified".)

Then Breen makes a comment about another specimen, and I quote: "Earl Parker had another one, offered in the Guggenheimer sale in 1953. Doubted, as mintmark is oddly shaped and obscured by a defect. Entirely different dies from any of the others."

Stack's wrote me about that Guggenheimer piece. They said it was

Researching the 1894-S Dime

withdrawn from the sale as a fake (altered mintmark) and returned to Jim Kelly (Parker wasn't mentioned).

I have one more mystery of sorts before I end this subject.

Late in 1980, I received a letter from a lady in Minneapolis. Her uncle, Robert C. Fay, of Cleveland, Ohio, had died in February. In his possessions he had an inventory of a coin collection. Included was an 1894-S dime. According to her, there has been little communication between Fay and his Minnesota relatives, and it was quite a while before they knew he had died.

The Minnesota people were the heirs to his estate. When they got to Cleveland there was no trace of any part of the collection. "Other people had access to his home and to his safety deposit box before we did," she wrote. A close friend of Fay's confirmed that he did indeed have a coin collection.

The immediate question is this: Was Fay one of the "unnamed" collectors here and there in the list of owners? Dealers who sold the specimens know who bought them, even if the buyers wanted to remain anonymous. I know as I was once one of the "unnamed" intentionally. If he was, will the dealer who sold him the coin, or maybe bought it back from him, reveal himself. Maybe we can find out more about Fay's coin.

Question & Answer Forum

by Q. David Bowers   1992

Q. I am interested in getting three basic varieties of the 1792-1794 "Kentucky" token and wonder how rare they are—the Plain Edge, the Engrailed Edge, and the Lettered Edge. I already have a Plain Edge, as you might expect, but don't know what the possibilities are for getting the others. Once you give me the answer I will send you a want list and you can get them for me—but I want to know how rare they are first.—E.R.C.

A. Most often seen is the Plain Edge variety, as you undoubtedly know. I would estimate that well over 1,000 pieces of these are in the hands of numismatists. The typical grades are rather high and range from Very Fine through Uncirculated, with Extremely Fine to AU being about average. Often such pieces have glossy surfaces. The Engrailed Edge is the type with reeding at a diagonal and are very rare, much more so than the *Guide Book* would indicate. I estimate that no more than 20 to 30 of these exist, and this may be on the high side; the figure may be more like 10 to 15. We have handled very few of them over the years.

As far as the Lettered Edge goes, that usually seen is the variety with PAYABLE IN LANCASTER, etc. I suggest that this piece is somewhere between four and eight times scarcer than the Plain Edge variety, and at least a couple of hundred of them are known to numismatists. The PAYABLE AT BEDWORTH, etc. and PAYABLE I. FIELDING varieties are exceedingly rare, and fewer than a dozen are known of each. If you just want a single Lettered Edge variety, the LANCASTER should suffice, and will cost a bit more than the Plain Edge which you already have, but not that much more.

* * *

Q. I have always wondered about the origin of the practice of placing the year of minting on coins, yet I've never encountered an explanation of it in the various books I've read. Without the date on a coin, the rare 1894-S Barber dime and the common 1916-S Barber dime would be identical twins. We all prefer dates on coins. But what was the original reason that dates were placed on coins centuries ago, and who was the first to do so? Also, why do the nations of our own time, including the United States, continue this practice?

A. There are several questions embedded in your theory, and I will do my best to answer them in series. The original reason for placing the date on a coin was to distinguish one year's issue from another's, so that the central government authority issuing the coins could distinguish the production of particular Mint officials. This was done, most probably, in order to assure that any lightweight or debased coins could be attributed to a particular official's custody of the Mint, who would then be held accountable for the lightweight or low fineness.

There are, however, other reasons for placing dates on coins. For example, the city of Tyre on the coast of Syria and Palestine threw off the yoke of the Seleucids in 126/5 BC, and thereafter dated their coins from that year. This was done, clearly, to proclaim the city's sovereignty. Coins of the Ptomelaic Kingdom of Egypt regularly bore dates, but these were nothing more than the year of the reign of the particular monarch issuing the coins. Since most Ptolemaic kings called themselves Ptolemy, and since each dated his coins from the start of his reign, it is often the case that two coins both bearing the same royal name and date were issued by two different kings, making attributions to a particular reign very difficult, if not impossible!

It is unknown to us as to who placed dates on coins first. Early issues of the city of Tyre, from the late 14th century BC, are dated, for example. These must be counted some of the earliest. In Europe, the Norman conquerors of Sicily dated their coins according to the year of the reign of the particular king. The Arab started dating the year in which the Prophet Mohammed left Mecca for Medina (AD 622). One of the earliest appearances of the Christian era dating on a coin can be found on the AD 1234 dated silver penny issued by Bishop Niels Stigsen of Roskilde.

By the late 15th century, European coins were more and more frequently dated in the Christian era. After 1501 most coins bore Christian era dates (at least, those issued by Christian rulers).

The United States continues this practice because the Mint is legally required to date coins in the year in which they were struck. Occasionally, as in the commemorative silver half dollar series, this legal requirement was not always honored. However, most modern countries carefully date their coins in the year in which they were struck. Since most modern nations' coinages are not struck in precious metals, the original purpose for placing dates on coins, as a quality control measure, is no longer applicable. Dates are retained on coins, today, for two reasons: 1. Because the public expects to find dates on their coins; 2. Because internal accounting procedures in most modern mints are based on calendar years.

***

Q. I really enjoy receiving your catalogues. I collect Mercury dimes and I noticed that some dimes cost more than others when the price should be equal. For example, the 1921 dime has a mintage of 1,230,000, but the May 1991 PCGS *Population Report* for Mint State coins with full bands is 108 pieces, broken down as follows: one piece in MS-60 grade, two in MS-61, nine in MS-62, 21 in MS-63, 40 in MS-64, 23 in MS-65, three in MS-66, and one in MS-67. An MS-65 coin sells for around $4,500.

I also noted that the 1931-S Mercury dime has a mintage of 1,800,000 but the total population of Mint State coins with full bands is only 73. The break down is as follows: MS-62, five coins; MS-63, 12 coins; MS-64, 26 coins; MS-65, 23 coins (the same number as for 1921), MS-66, seven coins. The 1931-S sells for around $750. Why does the 1921 cost six times as much? The 1931-S must be a true bargain.—E.K.

A: You have fallen into the "Population Report trap." Population reports are excellent, *up to a point,* but the use of them must go with other numismatic information as well. Your question is a perfect representative of an inquiry we must receive at least twice a week.

In Mint State grade the 1921 dime is probably at least 50 times rarer than the 1931-S. Over a period of years I have had rolls of 1931-

S dimes—in fact the Treasury Department was selling these for a number of years after 1931 to collectors who wanted them—but I have never even *seen* a roll or a partial roll of 1921 dimes.

The *Population Report* would also indicate that 1921 dimes are more plentiful in MS-64 grade than in any other Mint State level, followed by MS-65. On the contrary, reality is that MS-60 1921 dimes are much more plentiful than MS-65 coins, by a factor of several dozen to one.

The reason for this discrepancy in the population reports is that people who have low-level Mint State coins are not as eager to certify them as those who have high-level coins, due to the cost of certification. Thus, owners of 1921 dimes who think they have a coin that has a chance of grading, say MS-64 or MS-65 are apt to send it in for certification, while someone with an MS-60 coin won't bother.

Because the value of the 1931-S is low, fewer of these have been sent in. In fact, this is true of most Mercury dimes after 1930. We have a stock of several thousand Mercury dimes after 1930, and only relatively few of these have been slabbed.

Further on the subject of reports issued by various certification services, you could probably check—I haven't done this myself—and find that fewer Proof 1990-S cents have been slabbed than have Proof 1895 Morgan dollars, and yet a 1990-S is worth less than a dollar and a Proof 1895 Morgan dollar is worth $20,000 to $30,000. Reality is that Proof 1990-S cents exist by the millions, but few people have bothered to slab them. On the other hand, only 880 Proof 1895 dollars were struck, they are very valuable, and probably somewhere in the range of 20% to 30% of those in active numismatic hands (not counting those in museums and old-time collections) have gone the slabbing route.

As time goes on, more in-depth reports will be written on various series, just as Larry Briggs did recently for quarter dollars, in his book *Liberty Seated Quarters* (available from our Publications Department). Such references use reports of certification services as a *guide* to determining the availability of coins at *certain levels,* but not at others. For example, population reports would be very useful in finding out about coins in MS-60 or better. A detailed study such as Larry Briggs has done "brings it all together" and incorporates such data with information from other sources. This is what I am endeavoring to do with my new silver dollar book, and this is what has been done in a number of series—perhaps large cents 1793-1814 being the most outstanding example.

Trade Dollars

by Q. David Bowers   1993

The following was written for "The Joys of Collecting" column in COIN WORLD, 1993.

During the past two years I have come to "know" trade dollars quite well. In the course of researching everything I could find on the subject, as part of the groundwork for my book, *Silver Dollars and Trade Dollars of the United States*, I started by reading from cover to cover John M. Willem's magnum opus, *The United States Trade Dollar*, published by Whitman in 1965. In my opinion, this is one of the finest books ever written on *any* American coin series. Willem brings the trade dollar to life, and showcases it as one of America's most historical and interesting denominations.

In the course of delving into trade dollars, I was struck by the realization, in retrospect quite obvious, that these large silver coins were minted in nearly the same era as the popular Morgan dollar series, are every bit as interesting (as Willem notes), and are for the most part *much rarer*—but are virtually neglected by collectors. This is not as it should be!

Considering the business strike issues in the trade dollar series (and not the special Proofs made for collectors), the series has just one rarity: the 1878-CC. Even it is not all that expensive in the overall scheme of current pricing. The latest *Guide Book* gives these values: VG-8 (I have never seen one in such low grade, however) $300, F-12 (ditto; I haven't seen one of these either) $475, EF-40 (the usually seen grade range) $1,250, and MS-60 $6,000. EF-40 seems to be a nice compromise grade offering high quality and a reasonable price. Of course, a Mint State 1878-CC is even better, but only a few dozen exist at this level.

Each of the other dates and mintmarks is listed in EF grade from $135 to $575. A complete set of business strikes by date and mintmark includes the following:

1873, 1873-CC, 1873-S, 1874, 1874-CC, 1874-S, 1875, 1875-CC, 1875-S, 1875-S over CC, 1876, 1876-CC, 1876-S, 1877, 1877-CC, 1877-S, 1878-CC, and 1878-S—a total of 18 coins.

As noted, the only rarity is the 1878-CC. The 1873-CC is quite scarce, but at $350 for an EF, it is certainly affordable. 1875 is likewise scarce, but, perhaps, is a bit overrated in this regard. 1877-CC is scarce. In the common category are such issues as 1875-S, 1876-S, 1877, 1877-S, and 1878-S.

Looking for something interesting to collect? A series with a challenge? A series that is quite affordable? Consider trade dollars!

A Fabricated NE Sixpence

by Andrew W. Pollock III RCR 80 1990

After having carefully studied the Spanish colonial one-real counterstamped coin, with NE on one side and VI on the other, the author concluded that the counterstamps matched those of the NE sixpence illustrated in Sydney P. Noe's monograph, *The New England and Willow Tree Coinages of Massachusetts*, Plate II, -4 (referred to hereafter as Noe-4). This identical variety is listed as -10 in Walter Breen's *Encyclopedia*.

Both Alan V. Weinberg and Michael Hodder closely examined the piece and confirmed the Noe-4 attribution, although Mr. Weinberg's observations indicate that the punches were re-engraved between impressions of different examples, and Michael Hodder notes that NE and VI were strengthened on the coin by tooling.

The most intriguing feature of the coin is the undertype. It is interesting because it suggests to the author that the piece was made no earlier than the latter half of the 18th century, and probably considerably later.

On the NE side of the coin, if NE is held at 9:00, it is possible to see IND at 5:00, suggesting the Spanish origin of the undertype. The lower-left quarter of the shield is discernible, showing a lion rampant facing left. Part of the left border of the shield is visible, as is the line separating the lower-left quarter from the upper-left quarter. The left border of the shield appears to be vertical.

After searching through *Monedas Españolas Desde Juana y Carlos a Isabel II 1504 a 1868*, by Calico and Trigo, and through *Las Monedas*

Españolas Desde Don Pelayo a Juan Carlos I años 718 a 1979 by Cayon, the reverse design type which appears to best match this piece is that which appeared on Spanish colonial one-real pieces issued in 1772 and later, during the reigns of Carlos III, Carlos IV, and Fernando VII. The design has a shield with vertical sides and IND below.

The Noe-4 NE sixpence has long been a controversial issue. In 1943, Sydney P. Noe described and illustrated the variety in his *The New England and Willow Tree Coinages of Massachusetts*, but did not challenge its authenticity. Later, in 1959, Eric P. Newman, after having carefully studied the only specimen then known, pronounced it to be a fabrication. He argued that the piece was overweight, that the "NE and VI punches were back to back, contrary to striking practice employed at the Massachusetts Mint," and that although the coin was worn and scraped, the punch marks were sharp and unblemished. It is worth noting at this point that the Bowers and Merena specimen shares these same features.

Despite the strength of Mr. Newman's arguments, some numismatists have considered it to be a contemporary circulating counterfeit, and it is possible that some may still regard it as being authentic. Clearly, the evidence provided by the undertype of the Bowers and Merena specimen should lay to rest any vestigial belief that the issue is an authentic production of John Hull's 17th-century Massachusetts mint, or, for that matter, even a 17th-century counterfeit.

Regarding the possibility that the Noe-4 issue was counterfeited for circulation, we can only point out that NE sixpence were coined only in 1652 and probably were never common. By the late 18th century, it is likely that few people would have been at all familiar with them, and hence it would have been a poor choice for anyone who wished to counterfeit coins for circulation. Moreover, since the planchets of at least two of the known specimens are overweight, there would have been no financial advantage to the counterfeiter.

The most likely scenario is that the variety was created in the 19th century or even in the 20th century. Old, heavily worn Spanish one-real pieces were first scraped and dented to disguise the undertype. The resulting "planchets" were then struck with the NE and VI counterstamps. Any weakness in striking was then strengthened by tooling. The coins, most likely, were then sold into various collections.

Only three specimens of the variety can be presently traced:
- The Newcomer, T. James Clarke coin. 38.3 grains. Illustrated in the Noe monograph and the Breen *Encyclopedia*.
- The Smithsonian specimen, ex-Norweb Collection.
- The Bowers and Merena coin, 39.2 grains.

The author extends thanks to Michael Hodder, Eric P. Newman, and Alan V. Weinberg for their assistance in the preparation of this paper.

Let's Hear it for the Collector

by Q. David Bowers

The following article originally appeared in The Coin Collector's Journal.

Let's hear it for the person who counts in our business—the **collector!** All too often in today's busy market, transactions are accomplished on a dealer-to-dealer basis, with little thought given to the ultimate "consumer"—the *collector!* But you know, without the *collector* there would be no dealer-to-dealer transactions. Professional numismatists exist only as a conduit for transferring a coin from one collection to another. Dealers alone do not make a market.

My firm, Bowers and Merena Galleries, Inc., primarily deals with private *collectors*—private in the sense that they go about their collecting as a hobby, without publicity or fanfare. As I picture our customer in my mind's eye, I see a man (for most *collectors* are men, and I cannot understand why more women are not coin collectors), reasonably successful, in his twenties or thirties (or perhaps even in retirement), who has other interests, but who buys coins for **enjoyment.** I'd also say that my company is unusual, inasmuch as we primarily sell coins to people who enjoy buying them for artistic, romantic and historical purposes—*in addition to* being a store of value. We do not emphasize *investment* on its own, but suggest that the potential for profit exists along with the satisfaction of building a fine collection and holding it for a long period of time.

I have found that other dealers who emphasize investment in their sales presentations are apt to mortgage the future for the sake of a good sale today. A typical "pure" investor—the buyer who acquires coins for investment only and for no other reason—is apt to be a very fickle, difficult-to-satisfy individual. First, he seldom knows what he wants or why he is buying it (this is usually seen as an advantage, since recommended coins are always in stock!). Responsive to sales pitches, the typical investor tends to buy what is recommended, and does little serious research. On first acquiring a coin or group of coins, there is temporary satisfaction with their beauty and with the knowledge that they *are supposed to be* a good investment.

However, as there are no other considerations to sustain his interest except for the price alone, sooner or later he will wonder how his investment is doing. If it has stayed the same or has gone down—and that has happened for much of the market during the past two or three years—he is an "unhappy camper." No longer does he want to buy coins—yours or anyone else's. He complains that coin collecting is "a bad field," he has "been misled," "coins are a poor investment," etc. All of the energy you spent gaining a customer is lost—he is no longer a buyer of coins.

His interest grows

Contrast the investor with the *collector* who buys (to pick a miscellaneous example) an 1873-CC trade dollar and studies it, realizing that this is the first year of issue of one of America's most historic coins. He will appreciate that the piece was struck from the Carson City Mint using silver taken from the Comstock Lode. And his interest grows. Even a well-worn 1873-CC trade dollar has a great deal to recommend it as a collector's item.

In a word, such a coin can be *fun* to own. When something is fun to own, the enjoyment tends to last for a long time. If, for example, you buy a Currier & Ives print for $1,000 and hang it on your living room wall, you cherish no illusion that it will be worth $1,200 a year from now. Instead, you enjoy owning it and displaying it. If you keep it for 10 or 20 years, and then sell it for $2,000, this is fine, and it makes the ownership even more pleasurable. However, in the meantime, you have enjoyed it for other reasons.

It is no secret that the coin market is at a watershed, a turning point. The investment market of the late 1980s, with its highly touted "Wall

Let's Hear it for the Collector

Street money," is history, and what few investors remain in the market are often bruised. The investment market, with all its hype and promotion and ridiculous prices, drove many *collectors* from the field, and many have not returned. What market strength there is today comes from those *collectors* who opted to stay, and most buy lesser grade coins and staying away from "investment quality" pieces (MS-65, Proof-65 and higher levels).

Many areas were unaffected by the investment boom, particularly areas in which little emphasis was placed upon high grades. Ideal examples are large cents and colonial coins—the market for these has never lost its momentum. These coins in all grades sell today for as much or more than they ever did, and the enthusiasm is intense.

To me, it is perfectly obvious that any dealer wanting to have a successful business should emphasize the pleasure of collecting, not the profits of investing. On our mailing list, there are clients who have been buying coins from me ever since the mid-1950s—over 35 years ago! Many of these *collectors* are just as enthusiastic now as they were then. Since many coins are expensive, the investment factor cannot be overlooked, of course, but its long-term potential goes along with the formation of a collection—and on its own, pure *investment* has little chance for short-term success.

Enthusiastic new customers

The easiest way to cultivate *collectors* is to sell books (writing them is somewhat harder, but more fun!). Helen Carmody of the Society for U.S. Commemorative Coins recently said that my book published last year, *Commemorative Coins of the United States: A Complete Encyclopedia,* had on its own created quite a few *collectors* of commemoratives. Another dealer wrote to say that for every dozen he sold, probably six or seven enthusiastic new customers resulted.

I am not trying to sell copies of my book here—for the book has sold very well on its own. However, I am suggesting that any dealer wanting to build his clientele can do so by first "pushing" the sale of interesting reference books. I would speculate that fully half of the members of the Professional Numismatists Guild have not each sold a total of $100 worth of books to their clients during the past year! Such dealers have no one to blame but themselves in their sales and profits are slow.

In addition to whatever financial success you achieve from encouraging new *collectors,* you will also develop a number of new friends. I *enjoy* my customers. It is always a treat when someone takes the time to write me a nice letter, or calls to ask a question about a 1793 large cent, an 1895 Morgan dollar—or anything else, common or rare. Friends have been called the greatest asset anyone can have. Certainly, here is another reason for developing clients who are *collectors.*

As a professional numismatist, what you do today can directly influence the course of the hobby. Sit and do nothing, and the market will decline, as will the hobby. Take an active part, sell books, give talks at coin club meetings, write articles, encourage an interest in coins among young people, and otherwise get involved—in short, **do your share**—and you will find yourself part of a dynamic hobby that will swell during the 1990s.

Reprinted with permission from The Coin Dealer Newsletter.

Hard Times Tokens

by Q. David Bowers   1993

The following was written for "The Joys of Collecting" column in COIN WORLD, *1993.*

Are you looking for something new to collect? Something that is interesting? Something that is inexpensive? Something with a story?

If so, I suggest that you explore the field known as Hard Times tokens. These copper tokens, mostly the size of a United States large cent, were privately struck from 1832 to 1844. Some of the more fascinating varieties date from 1837, when banks suspended the payment of coins, and these tokens were used as substitutes in the channels of commerce.

Today, collectors divide these tokens into several major categories:

1. Pieces with political messages relating to President Andrew Jackson, the U.S. Bank, Daniel Webster, and other timely topics of the day.

2. Tokens superficially similar to U.S. cents, with a portrait of Miss Liberty on the obverse, but with an evasive legend such as NOT ONE CENT on the reverse, to avoid the laws against counterfeiting.

3. Store cards bearing messages of advertisers. To me, this category includes some of the most fascinating pieces. Illustrated are many diverse items, including a cow, planing mill, tinware teapot, boot, plow, comb, etc.

4. Mulings or die combinations, some of them illogical. One of these joins an obverse for a Belleville, N.J. butcher (T.D. Seaman) with

a reverse intended for a Canadian copper sou. Others were struck later, in the mid-19th century, as numismatic curiosities, to the order of Charles I. Bushnell.

In the 1950s, I bought my first tokens in this series from William Pukall, of Union City, New Jersey, who advertised each month in *The Numismatic Scrapbook,* the leading coin collecting periodical of the time. For about $1 to $5 each, I purchased several dozen different varieties. Since then, I have bought and sold many rarities in the series, and several important specialized collections. They are always a pleasure to catalogue.

In keeping with the coin market, prices have increased over the years. However, even now it is possible to collect many different Hard Times tokens for $10 to $25 each, and great rarities for in the $500 to $2,500 range. By way of comparison, for the price of a Proof 1879 $4 gold stella, you could form one of the finest Hard Times token collections ever assembled.

In conclusion, I refer you to a really great book on the subject, available from your local dealer for $14.95: *Hard Times Tokens,* the new 4th edition by Russell Rulau.

Thomas L. Elder

by *Thomas S. LaMarre*   RCR 70 1988

Inside the luxurious Milburn house in Buffalo lay President William McKinley, dying from a bullet wound inflicted by Leon Czolgosz at the Pan-American Exposition. Clerks and stenographers, summoned from Washington to handle the heavy mail, stayed at the house next door. Across the street, an election booth and several tents sheltered the members of the press. A detachment of regular infantry patrolled the sidewalk.

The stables of the Milburn home became an executive office, complete with telegraphic apparatus. The telegrapher? Thomas Lindsay Elder, who had recently joined the American Numismatic Association and was buying and selling coins in a small way. Elder would achieve recognition as one of the leading dealers during the next half century.

Sponsored by Dr. George W. Heath and George W. Rode, Elder had joined the ANA in 1899, receiving membership No. 140.

"Our readers are always interested in those who, for one reason or another, take the more prominent roles on the Numismatist stage," the April 1903 issue of *The Numismatist* said, "and we are pleased this month to present them with the photograph of this promising young Pittsburg [sic] collector and dealer.

"Mr. Thomas L. Elder was born at Dayton, Armstrong County, Pennsylvania, on November 22, 1874, and there he received the rudimentary elements of his education, later attending the Park Institute at Allegheny, and Beaver College at Beaver, Pennsylvania. As a stenographer and telegrapher he ranks among the experts, and many of our readers will remember that he was the government telegrapher at the Milburn home in Buffalo during the time President McKinley lay there. We have before mentioned that he has been offered a salary of $5,400 as court reporter at Nome, Alaska. This salary still awaits him, but he is rather inclined to remain in a climate where the chances are better to keep warm, certainly until the ratio between gold and coal becomes higher than 16 to 1.

"Mr. Elder has been a collector and lover of all things collectible since he was 8 years of age, beginning with tobacco tags, of which he had several hundred. He is an enthusiastic lover of art, literature, and music.

"In numismatics his tastes tend toward the artistic and historic. At present his whole time is given to his coin business, which in a few years has developed to considerable proportions. This is mainly due to persistent and judicious advertising, honorable dealings with his patrons, and promptness, three elements so necessary to success in any business."

There were an estimated 10,000 active collectors of coins and medals in the United States and Canada at that time. Their cabinets represented amounts from several hundred dollars to many thousands. There were about 21 full-time and part-time coin dealers in the United States.

At the time Elder's biography appeared in *The Numismatist*, he conducted business at 238 Sheridan Avenue in Pittsburgh. One year later he moved his business to 32 East 23rd Street in New York City. The interests of the Elder Coin and Curio Corporation were as diverse as the name suggested. One store card described Elder as an "importer and dealer in ancient and modern coins, paper money, curios, cut gemstones, etc." Similarly, his house publication, *The Elder Monthly*, was devoted to things numismatic, archaeological, philatelic, historical, antiques, etc. (A one-year subscription cost 50 cents.)

Elder was not the only numismatist whose interests strayed from coins, medals, and paper money. For a time the American Numismatic Society was known as the American Numismatic and Archaeological Society, as many of its members also studied Indian arrowheads, mummies, autographs, and rare books.

Elder saw benefits in all types of collecting. In the January 1907 issue of *The Elder Monthly* he wrote: "The surest way to save your child from being a spendthrift both of money and of time is to get him interested in coins, or stamps, or old china, or antiques. The deeper a boy or girl becomes interested in such objects, the less inclination he will have in later life toward the prevailing evils of gambling, drinking, and wasting his time."

Elder was clearly a believer in the temperance movement. One of the more than 300 tokens he issued was inscribed: THIS MEDAL IS DEDICATED TO THE CITIZENS OF THE RUM-SOAKED CITY OF NEW YORK, WHERE MORE MONEY IS SPENT DAILY FOR DRINK THAN WOULD CLOTHE AND FEED ALL OF ITS POOR. Another piece warned: SOME OF THE EFFECTS OF RUM: REVELRY, ROWDYISM, RIBALDRY, RIOT, ROGUERY, REMORSE, RUIN.

"Howland Wood writes that a search in the bar-rooms will reveal a lot of parodies of the motto 'In God We Trust,' " Elder wrote in the October-November 1907 issue of *The Elder Monthly*. "Wonder if he spoke from personal observation?"

However, collecting was more than an antidote to rum and revelry. Elder's philosophy was summarized in a token inscribed MORE ENDURING THAN BOOKS OR CUSTOMS OR NATIONS: A COIN.

In *The Numismatic Philistine* Elder wrote: "The pursuit of collecting tends to make a man methodical and orderly in his habits, and if he be a student of history, the study of the courtly customs of other days should train him to be polite, deferential, and diplomatic. . . His constant handling of rare coins and bric-a-brac will give him a sense of touch so delicate that he will not sit down on your Louis XV settee with the force of a catapult, nor will he handle your delicate iridescent Greek glass as though it were a football."

The Numismatic Philistine reminded collectors not to take themselves too seriously. "There is a humorous side to numismatic pursuit which is so irrepressible that it even leaks into the staid solemnity of the seriously minded numismatic reviews," Elder wrote in October 1909. "To such we aspire to supply a welcome supplement in lighter vein.

"It seems to us as if there is enough to make up an occasional budget of pertinent pabulum which will delight the soul of rectitude and incidentally hand the hot-airmatist an occasional tap in the region of the 'solar plexus' but good-naturedly and with 'eau de cologne' scented kid gloves."

In addition to *The Elder Monthly* and *The Numismatic Philistine*, Elder published the *Elder Rare Coin Book* and the *New Premium Coin Book*.

As a result of a squabble regarding the presidency of the ANA, he also published *The Elder Magazine* (1909-11) as a rival to *The Numismatist*.

"When will the members of the Association awaken to the fact that some limit should be put upon the editorial comment of the official organ?" Elder said. "It is high time to run a blue pencil through some of the impertinent, not to say unauthorized, criticism such as was indulged in the recent issue. Is the official organ getting to be a numismatic 'yellow journal?' This is simply a protest; when we speak again it will be in a different tone."

There was no one to run a blue pencil through Elder's own publications. Caustic comments were scattered throughout his catalogues in the form of "notices." Collectors either loved or hated Elder, who was outspoken against anyone who did not share his viewpoints.

Elder had strong opinions about collectors and collecting. One of his articles, published in *The Numismatist* in 1915 (his feud had long been resolved), was titled "A Plea for American Token Collecting." The topic may have been self-serving, because Elder issued more than 100 different tokens and medals. One of them was a 1912 Wilson dollar, inscribed T.L. ELDER/NUMISMATIST AND MEDALIST.

Elder belonged to not only the ANA, but also the American Numismatic Society, the British Numismatic Society of London, and the Royal Numismatic Society of Great Britain.

For the American Numismatic Society, he chaired a committee working for the improvement of American coinage. He helped establish the New York Numismatic Club in 1907, but resigned as secretary in 1918 because of his duties as sergeant in the New York State Militia. He had joined the Veteran Artillery Corps of New York in 1917 for services in case of war.

Elder disliked the trend toward collecting coins by date, a method of collecting which the debut of Whitman coin boards in 1934 helped to popularize. He also thought that collectors placed too much emphasis on small coins and coins of low value and denominations.

Elder tried to sell his coin business in 1931 but found no takers. In 1938 he retired to Pleasantville, New York, where he conducted occasional mail-bid sales.

He took advantage of the 1941 ANA Convention to criticize date collecting and renew his plea for token collecting. "If this [date collecting] helps numismatics, well and good," he said, "only I do not believe such collecting marks the Alpha and Omega of coin collecting, because it does not and never will. Nor will its intellectual rewards be great, though it furnishes recreation and relaxation.

"A coin of Brutus points to history and notable events. The issuance of a small cent in 1941 does not. Nor does it contribute one iota to mental improvements or aesthetic beauty.

"There are a number of fields and numismatic opportunities beckoning to the new collector. One of these is the neglected token and medal field. These branches, even the American series, are most important, and I predict will gain many recruits, as they deserve. Our colonial and continental series is large and varied, presents an attractive and instructive field, and should be better patronized."

Clearly, Elder was out of step with mainstream collectors. How could he say that a 1941 cent does not point to history and notable events? What about Pearl Harbor, FDR's third inauguration, and the Mint's increased wartime output? No aesthetic beauty? Admirers of Brenner's design do not agree. Elder forgot that there are no "rules" in collecting. A collection of Lincoln cents is no less respectable than a collection of medals and tokens of Henry Clay (one of Elder's specialties). Elder was making the same plea he had made in 1915, though he himself had not produced a token or medal in 14 years.

Elder, known to collectors as the "Dean of American Dealers," died in 1948. The July 1948 issue of *The Numismatist* reported: "After two years of declining health, Thomas Lindsay Elder, 71, passed away May 11, at Travelers Rest, South Carolina. For over half a century he had been one of the country's leading coin dealers and his death, while not entirely unexpected, comes as a great shock to all who knew him.

"A native of Pennsylvania, he established himself as a full-time dealer in New York City about the turn of the century. His love for coins, his keen mind, and his dynamic personality soon won for him a coveted place in the coin dealing profession. He never relinquished it.

"He was a prolific writer and many of his articles will be found in past volumes of *The Numismatist*. He could, and often did, prepare a thousand-lot catalog in 24 hours. His memory was so good, even to dates, that it was rarely necessary for him to consult a reference book.

"He is survived by his wife, Ruth Compton Elder; one brother, Knox Elder of Algood, Tennessee; and several nieces and nephews. Interment was at Kittanning, Pennsylvania."

New Exhibit Ideas

| by Q. David Bowers | 1992 |

The following was written for the "Coins and Collectors" column in The Numismatist, 1992.

This commentary is a result of observations I have made at the last several annual conventions of the American Numismatic Association, particularly at the most recent one in August 1992. Although as a dealer I am usually busy at my bourse table, I always take time out to view the educational exhibits of coins, tokens, paper money, and other items. Unfortunately, this year I didn't have to spend very long—exhibits, although including some excellent displays, were rather sparse in number, and some categories were thinly represented, if indeed represented at all.

As nearly everyone has the desire to share with others and to "show and tell," I started wondering why the exhibits were so few. Here are some ideas to ponder:

Today, certified "slabs" by PCGS, NGC, ANACS, and others are part of the collecting way of life. And yet I recall seeing only a single slabbed coin among the exhibits at the ANA show this year. Perhaps people feel that slabs and exhibiting don't go together. This can't be true, for a couple years ago PCGS mounted its $10 million silver dollar exhibit consisting *only* of slabbed pieces. However, individual slabbed pieces at typical coin exhibits—at the ANA and at other shows—seem to be close to nonexistent. Perhaps somebody should break the ice by showing a set of Proof Liberty nickels or some other series in slabs.

This brings up another point. In recent years there have been very few exhibits of regular United States coin series. When is the last time a date set of Indian cents, or Peace silver dollars, or Franklin half dollars, or Standing Liberty quarters was shown at an ANA convention? And yet these series are the lifeblood of coin collecting as we know it. I remember seeing about 10 years ago a set of Liberty Seated quarter dollars at a major show. While some coins were Uncirculated and Proof, many, if not most, were in the Very Fine and Extremely Fine category, and some issues—such as the 1842 Small Date and 1873-CC Without Arrows—were not represented at all. I found the display to be very interesting, and mentioned this to the owner, who happened to be a client. He said that throughout the show people had been congratulating him on it—Liberty Seated specialists who had despaired of ever seeing Liberty Seated coins on display!

In the collection you already have you probably own the ingredients for a display. There is nothing wrong with showing a set of Lincoln cents, or Jefferson nickels, or Morgan dollars struck at the Carson City Mint.

In my opinion, here is the best of my ideas, ruminations, suggestions (indeed, if any are worthwhile): I suggest that a special section of next year's ANA exhibits be set aside for *single* numismatic items. That's right—an exhibit category and special section for just one coin, just one note, just one token, or just one numismatic catalogue or book. The requirements would be as follows:

1. Only a single item could be shown (or two identical varieties or types could be used to display both the obverse and reverse).

2. The item is to be accompanied by printed material, a written description, illustrations, reference books, and other material telling the "story" of the piece.

I suspect that there are many ANA members who would be very willing to exhibit a single coin from their collection, but who do not want to go through the difficulty of packing up and insuring an entire set or specialized category. Individual single-coin exhibits would be easy to manage by someone on the ANA staff who could set up the case to the owner's specifications. This would be much easier than having to arrange a whole series.

Off the top of my head here are some ideas for a single-item exhibit—just to get the ball rolling.

New Exhibit Ideas

▼ A 1964 Kennedy half dollar accompanied by copies of articles from *Coin World, Numismatic News, The Numismatist, Coins Magazine, COINage,* and other periodicals telling of the new issue and its release; by photographs of President Kennedy who is portrayed on the coin; by a picture or two of engraver Gilroy Roberts, who designed it—and possibly even a list of things that were going on in 1964 (What were the top movies? The top songs? The fads? National news events that year?).

▼ An obsolete bank note from the town of your choice, accompanied by some post cards showing the town in later years, information concerning the officers and directors of the bank (usually obtainable today from the state banking commissioner), an explanation of the designs used, etc.

▼ A 1903-O Morgan dollar. This piece, which catalogued $1,500 Uncirculated in the 1963 edition of *A Guide Book to United States Coins,* was once considered the rarest and most desirable of all Morgan dollars. Then a great hoard was released by the Treasury Department, and the value sank as low as $17.50 per coin. Since then it has risen. The coin could be accompanied by some back issues of the *Guide Book* showing prices, articles about the October 1962 Treasury release of dollars, and perhaps an article or two from the *Coin Dealer Newsletter.* If more is needed, then a picture of the New Orleans Mint, perhaps an enlarged photograph of the coin being displayed (in all instances photographs make numismatic items easier to observe), and a commentary as to what was happening in New Orleans in 1903, when the coin was minted (perhaps a book on New Orleans history would give you this information).

▼ A 1909 V.D.B. cent. Here is one of the least expensive of all American coins with a "story." An Uncirculated piece can be obtained in the $10 range—no need for insurance here! This coin could be accompanied by newspaper clippings telling of the release of the Lincoln cent in the summer of 1909, an article from *The Numismatist* about the controversial initials on the reverse, some biographical information about Lincoln, information about designer Victor D. Brenner, etc.

▼ A Spanish-American silver coin brought up from one of the wrecks, such as the *Atocha,* off the coast of Florida. Finding photographs and articles to go with the display would be a snap.

You get the idea. I have deliberately selected inexpensive things. Actually, at the other end of the price spectrum, single-coin exhibits have been around for a long time—witness the 1804 silver dollar and

1913 Liberty nickel which, from time to time, have occupied showcases on their own; or what is believed to be the finest certified Proof 1898 Morgan dollar, which was in a case by itself at the August 1992 ANA show.

If a single-coin exhibit is worth developing, perhaps an award could be given for the best in this category. In that way someone with a single 1909 V.D.B. cent or 1964 Kennedy half dollar would stand a chance of winning—even if someone displayed an entire set of similar coins nearby. The judging could be done on originality and the educational and interest value of the accompanying materials, as well as the quality (but not the value) of the coin itself.

As it is now, there are more ANA exhibit awards than there are items on exhibit to claim the awards! Time and time again, as a viewer of exhibits or as a judge, I have seen "first place" go to a category in which there was only one entrant or possibly two. At least the single-coin exhibit category would probably engender competition. We need to put *enthusiasm* back into the exhibits, and this would be a great way to to it.

The next time you go to an ANA show, wouldn't you like to see dozens of different individual coins, medals, tokens, notes, and other items, each with an interesting story? I know I would. I will volunteer to be among such exhibitors.

A coin that comes to mind as I write this is a worn 1860-O Liberty Seated silver dollar that I bought for $550 at the recent ANA show. The 1860-O in Very Fine condition may be a ho-hum coin, you say, and it is. After all, *Uncirculated* pieces are common. However, this is no ordinary 1860-O. Indeed, it may be unique, for it is boldly counterstamped twice on the obverse with a seal of the government of Costa Rica, used during the late 19th century when coins of various foreign lands were counterstamped by the Costa Rican government for circulation within that country. I showed it to several Liberty Seated dollar specialists at the show, and none had seen or heard of such a thing. Upon coming home from the show, I wrote a small article about it for *The Gobrecht Journal,* official organ of the Liberty Seated Collectors Club. I mention this particular coin to illustrate that often an inexpensive coin can be of great interest if its historical background is known.

Hopefully this article will stimulate others to come up with thoughts about improving exhibits. Perhaps some of these ideas will breathe new enthusiasm and life into one of the most significant features of our annual convention.

Aspects of Collecting

| by Hugh Cooper | RCR 76 1990 |

The following was adapted from a letter from Hugh Cooper, a constant reader and frequent correspondent.

I have noticed a few happenings recently in the coin market. The 1793 Sheldon-1 large cent you own has been sold. Also the King of Siam set has moved. The Dexter 1804 dollar nearly broke the $1 million barrier, but that goal has yet to be attained, but seems inevitable. Once the $1 million mark is crossed, then probably it will be repeated often. Thousands of folks make more than $1 million a year, and multiple millionaires are Rarity-1, as we would say in numismatics. If the current money boom continues, more and more exciting coins will be brought out for sale.

I recently compiled a list of books I consider to be worthwhile for the beginning as well as the advanced collector, and it is a tribute to the book section of the *Rare Coin Review* that it is difficult for me to mention a key numismatic source currently in print which you don't have available.

Something occurred to me some years ago, and I never got around to doing anything about it: The creation of a *Who's Who in Numismatics*. Some of your publications come quite close to this. Your *The History of U.S. Coinage* gives many interesting biographies, and I refer to it often. In fact, other books you have issued in connection with auction sales, such as those about Virgil Brand, Abe Kosoff, Walter Nichols, and the Norweb family are very valuable. I suspect that over the years you have built extensive files on this subject. Your book, *The American Numismatic Association Centennial History*, is a good addition to your previous efforts. Still, I hope that someday someone will be able to spend the time and effort to write a comprehensive book covering many hundreds of names. Meanwhile, anyone involved in the coin field should definitely read the books you have already published.

The other day I was watching the Donahue show and saw and heard an actor plugging a book he had written. Although I was not familiar with the actor beforehand, he said a most telling thing: "Everyone should write a book about what he does—what it's *really* like to be an actor, or accountant, or a doctor, or a stamp collector. Anything. Young people should have some way of finding out what they have ahead of them." I didn't know who this guy was, and if asked I would have said that he was a utility infielder for the Detroit Tigers. However, what he said was meaningful.

Recently I read about a coin club in Connecticut which had 52 members, of whom only seven subscribed to any coin periodicals. Several have copies of the *Guide Book* no more recent than the 1960s. Most do not own a grading book. That is not surprising to me at all. It seems logical that everyone should own a copy of the current *Guide Book*, subscribe to your catalogues, and receive a number of different periodicals, but I have since learned that many people don't take the time to read. Books, while a very valuable source of information, have errors and omissions and eventually become out of date, although *The Early Coins of America*, by Sylvester S. Crosby, published in 1873, still is standard in its field. One should also subscribe to commercial periodicals, the best known of which are *Coin World* and *Numismatic News*, but there are also valuable monthly magazines as well. Anyone involved in numismatics, even transitorily, should read a weekly periodical. Also valuable are dealer newsletters, such as your own *Rare Coin Review*. Beginners typically are more interested in buying coins than in reading, but more mature collectors sense quite rapidly that there are many variables in collecting, buying, evaluating, and seeking coins. I have found that one of the best ways to become aware of what is happening is to order catalogues from a dozen or more dealers. Some will continue sending them for a long time, even if you don't buy anything. Others, particularly those with larger catalogues, ask for a small fee.

Beginners and newcomers to numismatics do not typically gravitate

Aspects of Collecting

toward auctions. However, ultimately, every serious numismatic type should take an interest in auctions. For one thing, the greatest rarities and finest collections almost exclusively appear in auctions, and although one might not be in the market for the greatest rarities, that does not admire one from studying the way they are presented for sale. In the field of large cents, for example, it would be difficult to envision any collector being informed on values and availability if he did not subscribe to auction catalogues.

The best auction catalogues are sometimes better than the collections they describe, at least in the sense that they describe the coins accurately and provide excellent photographs, bringing together all of the coins permanently, while the sale itself disperses them.

An excellent example is your sale of the Frederick B. Taylor Collection of colonial and state coinages, which you offered in March 1987. There are 743 pieces of early American coinage gathered by one of the most quiet and methodical collectors in United States history. The result was one of the finest cabinets ever put together.

Well, while a student needs to own reference books and also own the Crosby, Maris, Miller, and Ryder books, he also needs the Frederick Taylor Collection catalogue with prices realized.

I still remember the cataloguer's comment in your Taylor offering of a New Jersey copper, Maris 23-R, in MS-63 grade with much original mint red remaining: "Not only is this believed to be the finest known example of variety, but it is one of the finest preserved of all New Jersey coppers." The text went on to say that Mr. Taylor bought the coin from Stack's in 1951 for $32.50, and that the cataloguer hazards to guess that, "We would not be surprised to have it realize over 100 times the price he paid." That would have been $3,250. But the coin did better than that. It realized $17,600, or 541 times as much as Taylor paid for it!

Surrounded with interesting books and magazines and a consistent program to read them, a collector will naturally desire to talk about what he has learned and the coins he has collected. One way to fulfill this desire is to join one or more area coin clubs. Some clubs will not be to your liking, for they may have weak programs, or in small clubs the members might not be your style. Or it might be too far away to justify travel. However, most local clubs offer enough to be worthwhile.

There are also regional and national clubs. In my experience, such organizations as the Chicago Coin Club, the Illinois Numismatic Association, and the Central States Numismatic Society are all enjoyed by their members, as are many other clubs.

Another extraordinary source for education and comradeship is the specialty clubs, most of which "meet" by mail and through the issuance of journals. Most of these clubs are younger than 20 years old. Clubs exist for copper coins, transportation tokens, Liberty Seated coinage, and many other specialties. The John Reich Collectors' Society, a relatively new group, has been very successful. It began with a specialty in early silver coins, most notably issues from 1794 to 1836, but recently it added gold to its list of concerns.

I would also like to mention the Numismatic Bibliomania Society, which was organized in 1980 to recognize, research, discuss, and celebrate numismatic literature.

Before leaving the subject of educational reading, there is one other thing that I would like to mention, a thing which truly fosters education. That is conversation with educated folks. Although genuine well-educated persons are definitely scarce, they show up almost anywhere.

Once I walked into a small coffee shop in St. Charles, Minnesota, and met a man who apparently had collected large cents in the early 1940s, and not since then. We discussed coins, and he talked with great familiarity of Hays, Doughty, Clapp, and Newcomb, but he had not heard of Newcomb's 1944 work on 1816-1857 cents, nor had he ever heard of Sheldon's book! He told me that he had never bought a large cent, that he had traded for them or had been given them.

From time to time he took his coins out to look at them, which reminded me of a passage in the Sheldon book which tells of those who take large cents out on Friday nights, put them on the kitchen table, and enjoy their designs, color, and other aspects.

Sometimes people think that all that is worth discovering has been discovered in numismatics, but what I have learned is that the more one learns, the more there is to be discovered. However, there is a lot of erroneous information out there. There seems to be no cure for gullibility or untempered optimism, or for greed.

Once again I have let myself ramble on to great lengths, but I hope you have found some of my comments interesting.

Maybe I will put together all my notes and recollections, sort out the lies, and embellishments, and set them down on paper—the aspects of collecting and studying numismatic material.

Buy, Beg, or Borrow These Two Books

| by Col. Bill Murray | 1992 |

We reprint the following review by Col. Bill Murray from Coin World, *May 18, 1992. We are very appreciative of Bill's fine words:*

I just finished a monumental task. I have read Q. David Bowers' *The American Numismatic Association Centennial History* (1,744 pages in two volumes) and *Commemorative Coins of the United States: A Complete Encyclopedia* (only one volume, but 768 pages).

Dave Bowers has written small, amusing *Bedside, Fireside* and *Lakeside, Companions* which provide light, though often instructive, reading. The ANA history and commemorative coins books don't qualify as light reading. The *History* weighs in at slightly more than 11 pounds, the commemorative book at 5.25 pounds. You can hardly call that pocket-size.

You may not call them light reading, but you can call them easy reading.

Dave Bowers writes in a relaxed conversational manner, neither talking down to us nor flaunting his numismatic knowledge, which he could easily do. His use of anecdotes for illustration of points has long been appreciated. He has a knack for holding the interest of his readers. Dave has the ability to express the results of his research so that it can be easily understood and used by those of us who don't have the skill, time, temperament or desire to do all that digging.

Skill of digging out

This skill of digging out what others have written (often unskillfully) and producing the essence of their dissertations deserves note. Nowhere does this facility evidence itself better than in the *ANA History*.

The Numismatist, the ANA's monthly periodical, provided the source of most of the information in the *History*. *The Numismatist* had its birth before the organization of the brainchild of Dr. George F. Heath. He first published *The Numismatist* under the title, *The American Numismatist*, in 1888. Heath proposed the formation of an American Numismatic Association in 1891, and in that year a group of numismatists met in Chicago and formed the association. The rest, as they say, is history. That history, Dave Bowers has condensed into two volumes.

Dave has woven in additional information from other sources to augment what the editor, ANA officers or members wrote that appeared in *The Numismatist*. Further, he has analyzed the material from *The Numismatist*, related it to events going on in the world, the status of numismatics in general, the condition of the ANA, and activities of people in the hobby. He has looked for causes and effects that reflect the history of numismatics in this country, not just the history of the ANA.

Memory and experience

During the early years of the organization, this interweaving of material from *The Numismatist* with other data involved research exceeding a mere rehashing of the material found in the journal. For later years, I don't doubt that much of this Dave was able to produce from his own memory and experience.

Any numismatist serious about American numismatics will have a copy of *The American Numismatic Association Centennial History* on his shelf. These two volumes represent a history of numismatics itself in this country during the last 100 years. Further, the economics of the hobby for that same time are exposed by the extraction of price lists and sales reports from *The Numismatist* and discussion of changes in collecting habits of collectors and how these affect the business of numismatics.

The Numismatic Literary Guild chose the *History* as its Book of the Year for 1991. Hardly had we returned home from the ANA 100th Anniversary Convention than we discovered Q. David Bowers had published another book, *Commemorative Coins of the United States*.

Commemorative Coins of the United States starts out with an "Introduction." If you usually skip the introduction of other books, don't do it this time. The "Introduction" leads you into the book and personalizes it as Dave gives some background of his interest in commemoratives and how and why he has organized the book chronologically.

The "Introduction" is followed by seven chapters whose titles delineate their content: "An Overview of Commemoratives" offers a bit of history; "Enjoying Commemoratives" starts out, "Commemoratives are *interesting,*" and proceeds to tell you why. "Coins and Minting," may be unnecessary, perhaps, for qualified numismatists, but it typifies the way Bowers provides all the detail needed for complete understanding of the subject. "Commemorative Grades and Prices," admits the interest all of us, not just investors, have pertaining to the value of our collections, and tells how these subjects are dealt with in this book.

"Market History" provides a logical follow-up to the preceding chapter. "Collecting Commemoratives" gives some useful guidance. Chapter 7, "How to Use This Book," should not be passed over lightly. Here you will find the information to easily and knowledgeably follow the presentations in the rest of the book which catalogues all U.S. commemorative coins up to the current year (1991). Chapter 8 catalogues silver and clad issues; Chapter 9 covers gold commemoratives; and Chapter 10, "The Future," does not predict what may come, but tells, as of 1991, some of the proposals currently under consideration.

There are three appendices: "Artists Biographies and Credits,"; "Index of Subjects on American Commemorative Coinage, 1948-1991"; and "American Arts Gold Medallions." Each catalogue entry offers the story behind the coin, indicating what it commemorates, why it was struck (always for money?) and personalities involved, numismatic details and statistical information.

A series of transition sections, "The Continuing Story of Commemoratives," may be missed by some since they are not included in the Table of Contents. Unfortunately, many people will use this book as a catalogue and never read much of the textual material.

Buy, beg, borrow (but please don't steal) these books. You should read them.

Minor Coinage of the 1870s

by R.W. Julian RCR 77 1990

One of the most interesting, yet little understood, areas of American numismatics is the minor coinage of the 1870s. That some of it is rare and some quite common is generally known, but the reasons are not. Many fanciful theories have been published concerning this era, but the truth itself is equally interesting.

The cent, three-cent, and five-cent coins were the minor coins being struck in the 1870s, although some earlier coins, such as the two-cent piece, copper-nickel cents, and even large cents, were still in use. By 1875, however, the old large cent was rarely to be seen, except in rural areas of the country.

The minor coinages of the 1870s were all a product of the Civil War and the great need for coined money that arose. During 1862 all of the silver and gold coins had disappeared from the channels of commerce, leaving only the lowly cent to bear the burden of circulation. So acute was the shortage of coined money that rolls of 25 and 50 one-cent pieces were used in place of quarters and half dollars.

By late 1862, however, the pressure on the cent was so great that ordinary people began to hoard the copper-nickel coins bearing the Flying Eagle and Indian Head designs. (This hoarding, by the way, is why cents of 1857-1864 are still so common in this country.) In April 1864 the law was changed so that the cent was now of bronze; tens of millions were struck and went directly to circulation.

The cent coinages of 1865 and later (1864 was saved somewhat as a first year of issue for this alloy) were not only coined in smaller numbers than in the early 1860s, but fewer were saved, as there were plenty of such coins around and no reason for hoarding.

Three- and five-cent coins (of copper-nickel) were introduced in 1865 and 1866, respectively, in an effort to ease the pressure on the bronze cent and two-cent coins. These two new denominations were also meant as a subsidy for Joseph Wharton, owner of a nickel mine in Pennsylvania; his lucrative market had been cut short when the government changed the composition of the cent to bronze in 1864.

Beginning in 1870 the government made a determined effort to put silver coins back into circulation for the first time since the summer of 1862. The first hesitant steps were with the dime in 1868, but by 1870 indications were favorable, and stronger attempts were made.

In 1873 the Treasury took the final plunge and ordered Mint Director Henry R. Linderman to put silver into circulation, whatever the cost; the public was tired of paper money and their irritation could easily translate into votes at the next election.

The attempt was touch-and-go for a while, but by the beginning of 1874 Linderman had succeeded, and silver coin once more flowed freely in the arteries of American commerce. It is interesting at this point to note that the whole operation was strictly illegal, as Linderman did not have the authority to pay out silver for greenbacks or "shinplaster" (notes under a dollar in value). Congress, accepting reality, passed laws in 1874 and 1875 making the whole operation legal. To have done anything else would have been tantamount to political suicide.

The sudden appearance of silver in the marketplace meant that minor coins, especially the three-cent nickel pieces, were now less wanted than before. Therefore, coinage of this denomination showed a drastic downturn beginning in 1870 and, except for 1873, stayed in that mode for some years. The coinage of nickels (five-cent pieces) was erratic, but generally held up well in the early to mid-1870's. The bronze Indian Head cent fared about as well as the nickel.

One of the odder functions of the Philadelphia Mint in the 1860s and 1870s was the "re-issue" of coinage. On the theory that "clean money is happy money," the Mint was responsible for cleaning large amounts of copper-nickel coins.

At the beinning of 1876, minor coins, especially the two copper-nickel denominations, began to flow back into the Treasury in ever-increasing numbers. Toward the end of 1876 the cent joined this stream, and by early in 1877 Treasury vaults were overflowing with these minor coins.

This overabundance had actually been foreseen in the Mint law of 1873, and the Secretary of the Treasury, John Sherman, had the authority to suspend coinage whenever he felt that this was necessary. In 1876 Sherman did just that to the three- and five-cent pieces, while cent coinage was interdicted at the end of January 1877.

Most of the attention in the past decades has been focused on the 1877 cent, with a coinage of only 852,500 pieces. Rumors abounded as to why the coinage was so small (after all, the mints were striking large numbers of silver coins!) but the bulging Treasury vaults were quite enough. One of the more persistent, but toally unfounded, rumors was the story that the government intended to coin cents from copper-nickel; the halt in 1877 was to allow such coinage to begin.

It was not until the late summer of 1878 that cent supplies had become normal at the Treasury and Sherman allowed coinage to resume at the Philadelphia Mint, the only institution then making minor coinage; San Francisco, the next in line, would not do so until 1908. Demand was still low, and thus the abbreviated 1878 cent coinage came in at only 5.8 million pieces.

Most collectors seem unaware of the fact, but coinage of five-cent pieces was helped by private "contractors" in the New York area in the early 1870s. Even Mint officials noted that several of the dates from 1870 to 1875 had been heavily struck by these anonymous helpers. In short, counterfeiters were at work, but few, if any, seem to have been caught.

The counterfeits may be deteceted by comparing the artwork to genuine pieces. The hub did not change for the official government issue, but the counterfeits have slightly different design work. The cent and three-cent piece seem to have been left alone, probably because of profit levels and ease of putting into circulation.

The coinage of nickels in 1874-1875 was actually the subject of a small-minded debate in the U.S. Senate. One John P. Jones, a senator from Nevada, claimed that a shortage of nickels on the West Coast caused shopkeepers to shortchange their customers; he wanted, and got, a 20-cent coin of silver to eliminate the problem.

The whole idea was nonsense, and Jones' real motive was a new denomination to use more of the excess silver then piling up in the West. Nickels were sent by the Philadelphia Mint to western states, but prices were generally higher (as were wages) and few were used.

If any shortchanging did occur, it must have been a rare or localized happening.

The cent coinage recovered nicely from the enforced halt in 1877-1878 and continued at a strong pace for the next several decades, with one exception. There was another minor interruption ordered by the Treasury in 1885, and the result may be seen in reduced coinages for 1885-1886.

The three-cent coin never really recovered from its enforced idleness of 1876-1877, despite a curiously large coinage in 1881. No explanation has been found for the million-plus coins of that year; it may well be that the Mint had an excess of blanks on hand and simply decided to use them up in a period of low coinage.

Coinage of nickels did not really resume in force until December 1881 (this coin was always more popular than its smaller brother), which makes the large 1881 three-cent coinage all the odder. The coinage of nickels was interdicted in early 1885 and did not resume until late in 1886, creating two of the scarcer coins of the period.

Proof coinages of minor pieces during the 1870s has always been an area of considerable confusion among numismatists, extending back even to that era. As early as 1880 dealers were promoting the 1877 "Proof-only" coinage of three- and five-cent pieces as rare, though this was hardly the case. Hoarding was considerable, however, and prices were higher because of this.

Beginning in 1864 or 1865, the Mint began to issue "minor" Proof sets, which by 1867 consisted of the cent, two cents, three cents, and five cents. These were soon called "nickel" Proof sets by Mint officials, to distinguish them from the regular gold and silver sets.

With an occasional exception (the introduction of a new design in mid-year), minor coins were always included in the regular silver Proof set and, after 1866, in the "nickel" set. The number of minor Proof sets made prior to 1878 is not available, although it is known that in some cases, such as 1873, several hundred minor sets were made for sale to collectors.

In all cases the number of minor Proof coins is in excess of the published figure for silver sets. For 1877 considerably more is known for the reason that the present writer read the letters of the medal clerk to see how many minor Proof sets were mailed to customers outside Philadelphia.

There were 260 sets sent out by mail; added to the known silver

Proof coinage of 510 sets, this indicates an absolute minimum of 770 minor Proof sets in 1877. However, there were also local sales, and this figure may be put at 100 to 150 pieces. We therefore may estimate, with a fair degree of certainty, that the correct mintage of 1877 minor Proof sets was in the 870 to 920 range, probably about 900.

The 900 figure, which is about as close as we will ever come, considering that most medal and Proof coin records were destroyed in 1925, holds true for all three denominations, not just the nickel or cent.

Those selling the pieces in the future will naturally insist on the 510 figure, making the pieces more rare than they are. Collectors will prefer the higher figure when buying, for obvious reasons.

The truth is that the 900 figure will not make the coins any more rare or common than they are at present. It does not make any difference if a million or hundred million coins were made; it is what exists now that counts.

Strictly Uncirculated coins (MS-65) of the 1870s, especially for the minor coins, are generally rarer than the Proof coins. Collectors in the 1870s tended to ignore the common Uncirculated pieces in favor of the Proof coins struck by the Mint. This situation has had a peculiar side-effect at the present, as some dealers attempt to sell "Uncirculated" specimens of the 1877 nickel which are actually nothing more than poorly-made (or harshly cleaned) Proofs.

Getting Started

| by Q. David Bowers | 1993 |

The following was written for "The Joys of Collecting" column in COIN WORLD, 1993.

The other day I was talking with a friend, a collector of old postcards, who expressed an interest in becoming a coin collector.

While I have always been an advocate of the tried and true "Buy the book before the coin" sentiment, reality is that many who enter our hobby want to buy some coins right away. My friend said that for starters he had $100 to spend, and asked me for a suggestion.

After pondering the situation for a few minutes, I came up with this idea:

Today in the coin market, for $100 or less, you can buy a very nice Uncirculated specimen of an 1882-CC, 1883-CC, or 1884-CC Morgan silver dollar. These coins are large, brilliant, lustrous, and quite beautiful. Made from Comstock Lode silver, they were struck at the Carson City Mint, which produced coins for only a short time in the late 19th century.

While Liberty Seated dimes, quarters, and half dollars, and Liberty Head $5, $10, and $20 pieces with "CC" mintmarks are very expensive in Uncirculated grade, not so with the 1882-CC, 1883-CC, and 1884-CC Morgan dollars. This is because at the time they were made, there was little call for them in commerce. Their production was a result of the 1878 Bland-Allison Act, and was politically motivated, not need-based. As a result, most of the mintages of these dates went into storage. Years later, beginning in the 1930s, they came out of hiding from the San Francisco Mint and the Treasury Building (Washington, D.C.) vaults, where they had been shipped circa 1911.

In 1964, the Treasury took stock of its remaining holdings, and found it had about three million Carson City dollars on hand. These were subsequently sold through a series of auctions held by the General Services Administration, as many readers will recall.

To an old-time coin collector, a Mint State 1882-CC dollar might appear common, as indeed it is. However, to an outsider, such as my postcard-collecting friend, such a "CC" dollar is very impressive.

My friend bought an 1882-CC dollar, then an 1883-CC, then an 1884-CC, too! Now, he is well on his way to being a confirmed numismatist, and at last report he was spending a weekend with the *Comprehensive Catalog and Encyclopedia of Morgan & Peace Dollars,* by Leroy C. Van Allen and A. George Mallis!

Perhaps this will give YOU an idea as how to start a friend in our hobby.

What is Important?

| by Q. David Bowers | 1993 |

The following was written for "The Joys of Collecting" column in COIN WORLD, *1993.*

Scarcely a day goes by without my mail including information on some aspect of history or collectibles. I am not referring to coins—for I am immersed in coin literature and correspondence every day as part of my business—but to other fields such as art, music, autographs, postcards, old books, pre-1915 film posters, or another of my varied interests.

Recently the latest issue of *The Collector* appeared in my mailbox. Edited by Christopher C. Jaeckel, this fine newsletter is published by Walter R. Benjamin Autographs, Inc., of Hunter, NY. I found the editorial material, directed toward autograph collectors, to be quite relevant to numismatics as well. Just substitute the word "coin" for "autograph" or "letter" and you will see what I mean:

"Every time a Lincoln letter sells for a gazillion dollars at auction, or the popular media extols the advantages, financial or cultural, of collecting autographs, we are besieged with newcomers to the field. Many are genuinely interested in the autographs themselves. Others may be interested purely, or primarily, in an autograph's 'profit potential.'

"The first question invariably asked is 'What should I collect?' or 'What is a good investment?' Our readers know that we are not fond of the term 'investment' in connection with collecting autographs. It is not that we are insensitive to the desire for collectors to avoid spending their money for something which, like a car, depreciates substantially when it leaves the showroom floor. Kept long enough, that car may well prove to be worth more as an antique than it was when new. But, for most people, the reason for buying the car in the first place is to provide transportation, *i.e.*, to satisfy a current need. So with the autograph collectors, we prefer not to build a portfolio in anticipation of future profit, but rather to satisfy the collector's interest in history or literature of science, to satisfy his need to learn more about a particular subject, event or hero...."

In coins, as in autographs, investment can be an important aspect to those who form collections with care and hold them for a long period of time. However, equally important, in my opinion, are the historical aspects, fascination, camaraderie, and pure joy of collecting that numismatics offers.

Join the Club

| by Q. David Bowers | 1993 |

The following was written for "The Joys of Collecting" column in COIN WORLD, 1993.

It's fun to belong to a common-interest group. Within numismatics there are many clubs catering to enthusiasts in various series. A short list includes the Liberty Seated Collectors Club, John Reich Collectors Society, Token and Medal Society, Society for U.S. Commemorative Coins, and Society of Paper Money Collectors. A dozen or more names could be added.

Each week as I write this column I am apt to be inspired, amused, or annoyed by something that comes to hand just as I sit down at my Macintosh computer to turn out these paragraphs.

Today, the latest copy of *Penny-Wise,* the journal of Early American Coppers, Inc., arrived in the mail. I dropped everything to scan the table of contents, and then spent the next half hour reading articles and commentaries of interest. The rest of the 94-page issue will await a leisure hour. I am reminded that the editor of *Penny-Wise,* Dr. Harry Salyards, is one of the few people in numismatics today who combines excellent technical know-how with the "big picture"—a familiarity with history, art, literature, and economics. How fortunate readers of *Penny-Wise* are to have him on board.

The Early American Coppers club is model of what a specialized numismatic group should and can be. While its journal deals with new discoveries, technical aspects, and notes on United States large cents and half cents, and to a lesser extent, colonial and state copper coinage, any reader of *Penny-Wise* knows that there is much more. For example, in the latest issue, once you are finished exploring the question posed by Jim Hart, "does an 11-star Sheldon-277 1808 large cent exist?" you can read the ANA Convention diary of Denis Loring, and learn that the sight of a mouse in an Amtrak car caused unexpected problems.

Early copper coins form the focus for what can be best described as a forum for the sharing of pleasures and information, the coming together of a thousand or more people to enjoy numismatics. There is no doubt that the typical member of EAC, as the club is called, has fun.

To find out more about the non-profit EAC, write to Rod Burress, Box 15782, Cincinnati, OH 45215. If you can't wait, send your check for $20 for a year's membership (just $5 if you are under 18 years old). I know you'll find membership to be worthwhile.

This & That

from Rare Coin Review Nos. 86 & 87 1992

TONY CETERA, a client in Japan, sent us an article from the *Mianichi Daily News* noting that in Switzerland a dress worn by Marilyn Monroe in the 1954 western film *River of No Return* was auctioned for the equivalent of $41,000 U.S. dollars. Tony then wrote: "Even though coin prices are down, I just bought a very beautiful 1883-CC $10 piece for $1,595—a great value. Coins are still underpriced compared to other forms of old art, such as old Japanese Imari porcelain, ukiyoe (wood block prints), Chinese porcelain, old ivory carvings, etc. Also, the chances of dresses, paintings, and the like being imitations are rather great, but when I buy coins from you I know I will never get an imitation coin. Best wishes and success in 1992."

* * *

A MINOR POINT CONCERNING GEOGRAPHICAL SPELLING: "Pittsburg was the official spelling for that western Pennsylvania town between the years 1890 and 1911. Pittsburgh lost the 'h' in its spelling when the U.S. Board of Geographic Names decided in 1890 that all towns ending in 'burgh' would henceforth end in 'g.'

"Years of complaints by city residents moved the board to reverse its decision, and Pittsburg got back its 'h' in 1911" (from the *Antique Bottle & Glass Collector*).

* * *

THE MORE THINGS CHANGE the more they stay the same—the following was from a Treasury news release: "United States Mint changes dating of American Eagle from Roman to Arabic numerals." The news item went on to say that a "more readable coin seen as more appealing to consumers" and that to change will "make the Eagle easier to read and more attractive for gift-type giving." The United States has tried Roman numerals a couple of other times in its history. In 1907 (MCMVII), which did not last even a year before the regular 1907 date was utilized in its place, and again for the short-lived issue of $50 commemorative gold coins in 1915 (MCMXV).

* * *

MARK GLAZER wrote the following: "I ordered from you and just finished reading *The Numismatist's Bedside Companion* and found it most enjoyable reading! I will be passing it on to a collector friend of mine." Another reader, a dealer from California, wrote about the same book: "I gave as a gift a copy of The Numismatist's Bedside Companion to a non-collecting neighbor of mine. He read it, bought three more books, and is now starting a coin collection. You and others are perfectly right when you say that reading about coins gets people interested in them!"

* * *

AN INTERESTING question from Albert S. Garczynski of Philadelphia: On which U.S. coin does the motto "E Pluribus Unum" appear twice? The answer: On the reverse of the Mount Rushmore silver commemorative dollar, designed by Frank Gasparro. It appears in the "Great Seal" and above the words "One Dollar."

* * *

A NOTE from Russell MacKendrick, numismatic writer, commented on a recent listing of ours offering coins slabbed in "ANA cache" holders—and wondered, humorously, whether the American Numismatic Association did indeed maintain a cache or hoard of coins. This brings up the question of the pronunciation of "cache." We have always pronounced it similar to "cash," but some others have pronounced it as "catch" or "caysh."

* * *

CURT WOOD, a Rare Coin Review reader, suggests that with so many new coin grades, there should be provision made for additional grades for pieces "worn down below About Good, and below Fair, and even down below Poor." He suggests that AE could stand for "Almost Extant," that ON could stand for "Oh, No!", and finally, BB, "the lowest possible grade in all of numismatics, would represent 'Bye Bye.' " Curt, why don't you forward your suggestions to the American Numismatic Association for inclusion in their next "Grading Guide?" Just kidding, of course!

* * *

SAM LUKES wrote to say that on the popular television quiz program, Jeopardy, a contestant was asked: "What is the name of the figure who appears on the 10-cent piece prior to the Roosevelt dime?" Sam stated that the contestant correctly answered that Liberty was represented, which, of course, most numismatists know. However, he was told on the game show that the correct answer should have been "Mercury" and that Liberty was incorrect. Sam wrote to the producers of the show, quoting from one of our books, United States Dimes, which states the following: "The issue was not intended to represent Mercury, the messenger of mythology with wings on his feet, but to represent an allegorical figure of Miss Liberty with wings on her head, to illustrate 'liberty of thought.' The design superficially resembled that of Mercury, at least the public made this connection." The powers that be at Jeopardy wrote back to say that they should have checked further, errors sometimes happen, but in any event the contestant would not have gone further anyway (an answer which Sam Lukes found a bit hard to believe). Readers of the Rare Coin Review may rightly remember a few issues ago when we showed a picture of Kathy H. Fuller, of The Johns Hopkins University, who was also a Jeopardy contestant, and who was given a second chance after the show called her right answer wrong. Perhaps the American Numismatic Association should send the producers of Jeopardy a membership application.

* * *

COMPUTERIZED COINS: Coin collecting as a hobby and investment received some good publicity recently in CompuServe Magazine, the publication for members of the CompuServe On Line computer service. The magazine noted that, "Nickel and dime stuff can lead to a worthy return—with a thorough grasp of the rare coin market." The on-line service offers member forums (computerized discussion groups) on such topics as numis-

This & That

matic trivia, weekly coin club meetings, forum price guides, and even on line auctions.

* * *

ORCHIDS TO the Isle of Man and onions to the U.S. Mint: The following is from an American Numismatic Association news release: The 100th anniversary of the ANA is commemorated on silver and gold legal tender coins issued by the Isle of Man. The ANA, which was founded in Chicago in 1891, is the first numismatic organization to have legal tender coins struck in its honor. . . ANA President Edward C. Rochette said, "This is truly an historic event and a great way to mark the ANA's first 100 years in world numismatics. On behalf of the entire membership and the Board of Governors, I wish to express our sincere appreciation to Derek Pobjoy, the Pobjoy Mint, and the Isle of Man for producing this special coin for the ANA's centennial."

The question is: Why couldn't have the U.S. Mint, right in our own backyard, have created a commemorative coin for the ANA centennial? It would have sold well, the cost of dies would have been quickly repaid, and a public relations coup would have been scored. We had a commemorative *stamp* marking the occasion, but no commemorative coin. What a shame! However, all is not lost—1992 marks the bicentennial of the establishment of the U.S. Mint in Philadelphia in 1792, and 1993 marks bicentennial of the first issuance of copper coins (cents and half cents) for circulation. How about it, Mint? Let's get to work and turn out some commemoratives for one or both of these occasions.

* * *

ANGUISHED ENGLISH: An interesting collection of signs in foreign countries, resulting from a flawed knowledge of English.

In a Japanese hotel room: Please to bathe inside the tub.

In a Paris hotel elevator: Please leave your values at the front desk.

In a Belgrade hotel elevator: To move the cabin, push button for wishing floor. If the cabin should enter more persons, each one should press a number of wishing floor. Driving is then going alphabetically by national order.

In a Leipzig elevator: Do not enter the lift backwards, and only when lit up.

In a Yugoslavian hotel: The flattening of underwear with pleasure is the job of the chambermaid.

In a hotel in Athens: Visitors are expected to complain at the front office between the hours of 9 and 11 am daily.

(Thanks to Cheri Lemons for sending us this column from MIND, the newsletter of Indiana Mensa.)

* * *

SPECIAL THANKS to Al DeForno, who read through the several different titles of our "Companion" book series and sent us detailed ideas for corrections. These will be incorporated in future printings. Thanks again, Al.

* * *

WHAT does this comment mean? "It may be an unfair statement, but City Park in New Orleans was so beautiful and well maintained that it is difficult to conceive that it is managed by municipal government." (from *The AMICA News and Bulletin*)

* * *

ELECTION YEAR optimism: Mike Fuljenz recently wrote in *Coin World* an article which noted that in presidential election years since 1964, headlines in the *Coin Dealer Newsletter* (which was first published in 1963) showed optimism, which depended on politics: "Every four years, the incumbent administration in Washington does whatever it has to do to kick-start the economy." Quoting an article by Richard Hoey in *The Wall Street Journal,* Mike went on to say: "It works like a clock. Political and economic officials will sacrifice any principle and break any rule to get an economic recovery in an election year." Selected titles from *The Coin Dealer Newsletter* in election years in question:

"1964: Bidding increases in active market; 1968: Bidding active, gains everywhere; 1972: Advances continue across entire market; 1976: Entire market active, plus signs are everywhere; 1980: Type coins soar to new record levels; 1984: Dollars, commems, type, all score advances; 1988: ANA: Type advance accelerates."

Mike Fuljenz didn't mention that these also were leap years—perhaps the whole thing has to do with astrology and not with politics!

* * *

THE MOST INTERESTING lead paragraph in an article seen recently: "Although it is too early in this article to discuss orgies, suffice it to say that sea slugs are much more interesting creatures than they might at first appear." (From a front page article in *The Wall Street Journal*)

* * *

LETTER FROM THE IRS TO A TAXPAYER: "Please advise us of the date of your death." (as quoted in *Newsweek*)

* * *

SEEN RECENTLY on the cover of a publication: "All roads lead to SIN." No, it wasn't a religious publication, nor was it a guide to the steamy side of life, but, rather, it was the latest journal of the Society for International Numismatics, which takes pride in its S.I.N. initials and, in fact, uses two devils as *part* of its organization emblem. "Serving the numismatists of all nations," the organization's mailing address is Post Office Box 943, Santa Monica, CA 90406-9430.

* * *

THE OTHER INDEPENDENCE HALL is located in Buena Park, California, according to a recent article by Alan Herbert in *Numismatic News*. "Built by Walter Knott at Knott's Berry Farm, it also has a replica of the Liberty Bell. This is authentic right down to the crack, created by the freezing the bell in dry ice and then applying the intense heat of a heliarc welding torch. The second, identical Independence Hall replica is complete with an original copy of the Declaration of Independence." Now, is there a second Washington Monument somewhere?

* * *

BOOM TIME IN CRIPPLE CREEK: The last time there was frenetic activity at Cripple Creek, Colorado, high in the Rocky Mountains behind Pikes Peak, was in the 1890s and early 20th century when this was for a period the richest gold district on earth. After that the population diminished from an estimated 50,000 down to about 750 a few years ago. Enter legalized gambling, which became a reality in 1991. We heard one person who had a store on Bennett Avenue (the main street of Cripple Creek) and who sold it for $30,000 a few years ago recently heard that it had changed hands again for $600,000. In Victor, a few miles away from Cripple Creek, where gambling is also legal, there is a rush on real estate, and word has it that the American Numismatic Association is getting several hundred dollars a month by renting the house formerly owned by Joseph Lesher (distributor of Lesher silver "dollars" in 1900-1901) which was donated to the ANA a few years ago. The Lesher house is the oldest numismatically related building still standing in the state.

* * *

DON KAGIN sent a surprise envelope the other day stuffed with old catalogues Dave Bowers sent to his father, Arthur M. Kagin, many years ago—some of them dating back to 1956. Thanks, Don. It was nice to look through all of these old catalogues again—there were nice memories.

6,000-Year-Old Advice

by Weimar W. White   RCR 79 1990

One of my favorite books on the subject is *High Profits From Rare Coin Investments*, 12th edition, by Q. David Bowers. The book is a must for collectors who want to assemble a valuable coin collection with capital appreciation potential and learn about the history and romance of the era they represent at the same time. In reading Dave's book, one comes away with a much better understanding of the forces that drive the coin market and how to avoid the pitfalls while building your collection.

In the Facts and Figures section, a price appreciation review is given starting with 1948 to 1989 for 127 classic U.S. coins of copper, silver, and gold issues, plus colonials and commemoratives. Most of the coins represented are in MS-60, with the prices taken out of *Guide Book* issues during the 41-year time span.

Although not specifically mentioned by Dave, the average annual compound rate of return for this cross-section of diverse coins is 12.43%. At this rate, the coins, as a unit, would double in value about every six years. Not a bad performance for numismatic properties in mostly MS-60 condition!

This brief review of Dave's book brings us to the primary purpose of this article, and that is the financial thinking of the wealthy men of Babylon about 6,000 years ago. History tells us that Babylon was the wealthiest city known during its thousands of years of existence. This is because the successful members of society appreciated money

(Babylonians are believed to be the original inventors of money as a means of exchange) and understood its value and its laws. Could it be that some of us in today's world have forgotten the financial wisdom of the ancients?

From the book, *The Richest Man in Babylon*, by George S. Clason, 1955, The Five Laws Of Gold are listed. These laws describe what the ancients knew of money management back then (BC).

I. "Gold cometh gladly and in increasing quantity to any man who will put by not less than one-tenth of his earnings to create an estate for his future and that of his family."

II. "Gold laboreth diligently and contentedly for the wise owner who finds for it profitable employment, multiplying even as the flocks of the field."

III. "Gold clingeth to the protection of the cautious owner who invests it under the advice of men wise in its handling."

IV. "Gold slippeth away from the man who invests it in businesses or purposes with which he is not familiar or which are not approved by those skilled in its keep."

V. "Gold flees the man who would force it to impossible earnings or who followeth the alluring advice of tricksters and schemers or who trusts it to his own inexperience and romantic desires in investment."

Well, this is quite a lot of wisdom so simply put. The reader may ask, what does all this have to do with building a coin collection having good investment potential? Let's start with the first law. It is telling us to learn to live on 90% of our take-home pay and to invest the remaining 10% wisely in diverse vehicles, i.e. stocks, real estate, coins, etc. Sure, this is hard to do, but if one invests first and then pays the bills, it can be done.

The second law describes what is known as the "eighth wonder of the world," and that is the way compound interest multiplies one's wealth. As an example of this principle given in Dave's book, we see $5,115.75 invested in the 127 coins in 1948 is now valued at $624,033 41 years later. This corresponds to an average annual compound growth rate of 12.43%.

The third law states that to keep wealth, one should seek out those who have a good reputation in knowing how to preserve and make capital grow. This concept requires some homework on the part of the investor.

6,000-Year-Old Advice

The fourth law is very important to the beginning coin collector. In numismatic terms, the writer would sum it up this way. Before one jumps into spending money on coins, first build yourself a small library of books relating to the area of numismatics for which you are most interested.

The last (but not least) law advises us not to run after returns that are unrealistic. Here is where one should suppress his greed urges. For example, there are many schemers out there who would try to convince you that a coin or some other entity will double or triple in price in a year if it is purchased now. 100% or 200% returns on investments seldom happen with regularity. And more often than not, the person who follows this kind of advice will be a loser in the long run.

In summary, this article is meant to show that money today is governed by the same laws that the people in Babylon used 6,000 years ago. To be successful in the management of one's finances, some very basic principles still apply.

Improvements at the Bureau of Engraving and Printing

by Day Allen Willey

The following article is excerpted from the December 12, 1914 issue of Scientific American.

A building that has been an eyesore of our capital was the Bureau of Engraving and Printing, where much of our currency is made. For years, workers have been crowded together in hot, dirty rooms, the floors greasy and stained with oil and littered with scraps of paper. The law compelled them to remain within the building for the entire day, for fear some employee might steal the valuable paper on which the bank bills are printed. Consequently, all the workers had to bring their noon lunches with them and eat within the Bureau, finding a place where they could sit, such as an empty box, a stool, or perhaps the stairways leading to the rooms.

Uncle Sam has at least given thought to these careworn moneymakers and has provided a building for this bureau that is one of the most attractive in Washington, and is really a factory home in the many provisions made for the comfort of those who labor within its walls. The new structure consists of a main building of sandstone, and the sides and ends of the wings are devoted almost entirely to windows, with the glass set in metal sashes. It has been estimated that 32,000 large panes of glass are required for the windows of the buildings.

The total floor area of the building is 476,700 square feet, and the cubical contents are about 7 million square feet. In planning this new factory, especial attention has been paid to the health and well-being of the employees.

A man who is well-fed is in better condition to render good service than he who is in need of proper nourishment. Hence the installation of a cooperative lunchroom in the new building. It is the duty of the physician in charge to supervise the sanitary conditions of the establishment. Each day he inspects the entire building, enforcing the utmost cleanliness, insuring every employee the necessary amount of ventilation in the room in which he works, studying light conditions and relieving eye strain. In addition, he is always present to administer first aid to any case of accident or relief in lesser ailments. In the new building pamphlets will be issued relating to the special illnesses likely to be met within this sort of work.

It has been planned that the employees shall operate the lunchrooms themselves. The government has furnished all the necessary equipment, with the exception of dishes, silverware, linen and such accessories, which will be provided by the employees. An association of the workers has been formed for the purpose, women employees subscribing 50 cents each and the men $1 each. In this manner, a fund of $2,000 has been raised. It is planned to refund the subscription as soon as the finances will permit. The lunchrooms are not to be operated as money-making propositions, and the food will be sold at the lowest possible figure.

Another advantage of the new bureau is that all of the mechanism is operated by electric motors, except the preliminary work.

The methods of turning the sheets of linen paper into bills have been greatly improved in the new plant. First the sheets are dampened so that they will take a good impression from the printing press. Then they are placed upon presses, where lettering and other characters are placed only upon the back. From these presses the sheets are taken to steam driers, where they are dried to set the printing ink. But before anything further is done, the sheets must again be moistened, after which they go to the electric printing presses, and the front surfaces are lettered and stamped. After a further drying in the steam chests they are put upon the machines which place the number of each note in the proper position upon it.

The partly finished money is now ready for the counters. These are all women, and the rapidity with which they work is really wonderful, as the visitor sees them picking up sheet after sheet so rapidly that he can hardly distinguish one sheet from another. The counting is done to make sure that none of the money sheets have been lost or destroyed in any way; and after it is completed, the currency in the form of sheets, each containing from four to eight notes, is ready to be carried in the big wagon to the Treasury.

Experiments with Aluminum Coins

by Thomas S. LaMarre

Danish chemist Hans Christian Oersted produced the first aluminum in 1825, but it was considered an exotic metal until cheap electrochemical production processes were developed in the 1880s. Long before then, various nations began experimenting with aluminum coinage.

In 1855 an aluminum ingot was displayed at the Paris Exhibition, and all sorts of uses were envisioned for the metal. However, coinage did not seem to be one of them.

"It has been said that aluminum may someday replace gold and silver in our coins," *La Presse* snickered. "Aluminum can never be destined for such use. In fact, that which contributes to gold and silver the special characteristics of precious metals, that which has determined their choice for this purpose, is the facility with which they can be withdrawn from their alloys and reconverted into pure metal.

"By very simple chemical operations, gold and silver are extracted in the pure state from any combination in which they may occur. Aluminum is unfortunately without this property; it cannot be separated in the metallic state from its diverse compounds. In place of aluminum, the attempt yields only alumina, the common base, without any particular value.

Sign of wealth

"Such a circumstance prevents the use of aluminum along with silver and gold in our coins. Further, a metal of such common occurrence, forming a large part of the clay which we literally tread under our feet, and whose value may vary from all sorts of circumstances, can in no case be accepted as the representative sign of wealth."

Nevertheless, Henry Montucci, a member of the French Academy of Sciences, foresaw the day when aluminum would indeed be used for coinage. Its advantage, he theorized, was that it would end the practice of melting silver coins to obtain the higher value of bullion. (The U.S. government attacked this problem by reducing the weight of all silver pieces, excepting the dollar, in 1853.)

In 1855 the U.S. Mint struck a pattern aluminum half dollar. Three years later, J.L. Bell began making aluminum near Newcastle, England, but the plant soon closed because of lack of demand.

In 1863 U.S. Assayers Adam Eckfeldt and William Dubois recommended the production of an aluminum coin, perhaps as a means of dealing with metal shortages brought on by the Civil War. Chief Engraver James B. Longacre produced several patterns in aluminum during the next few years. These were considered quite pleasing and Longacre suggested that all denominations of silver coins be made with 5% aluminum content instead of copper. The resulting coins would be as hard and durable as those containing copper, he said, but would have a more attractive color.

Although his proposal was rejected, Longacre continued to experiment with aluminum patterns. "The use of aluminum for the purposes of coinage was suggested by its peculiar qualities as I became acquainted with them," he explained to Secretary of the Treasury Hugh McCulloch.

In 1868 Longacre produced sets of aluminum patterns containing examples of all 16 denominations. These were packaged in custom leather cases and presented to Mint Director Henry R. Linderman. In 1873, Linderman presented a six-piece pattern trade dollar set, struck in aluminum, to Secretary of State Hamilton Fish. (Wayne Gretzky of the Los Angeles Kings hockey team purchased this set for $137,500 a couple of years ago.)

In 1883 the London Royal Mint conducted a series of tests with regard to the wearing qualities of coins of assorted alloys, including aluminum. Fifty coins of the specified metals were placed into a tumbling barrel and weighed after six hours and again after seven hours.

As was probably expected, coins comprised of 98% aluminum, 2% nickel showed the least wear in terms of weight but the most wear

Experiments with Aluminum Coins

relative to the percentage of the coin. When the Royal Mint tested an alloy of aluminum and gold in 1891, it learned that the color ranged from yellowish green to purple, depending on the percentage of aluminum. Mint technicians also found that an alloy of 10% aluminum, 90% gold has a melting point lower than that of aluminum alone, and that an alloy of 22% aluminum, 78% gold has a melting point several degrees higher than that of gold.

This type of testing was fine and good, but many people wanted aluminum taken out of the laboratory and put into practical applications. At the 1894 American Numismatic Association convention in Detroit, D.C. Wismer urged the U.S. Mint to strike aluminum coins:

"The supply (of aluminum) is practically unlimited. It constitutes one-tenth of the earth, being most abundant in clay. It is a white metal somewhat resembling silver, is very malleable and ductile, in tenacity nearly the same as iron, and takes a high polish. When exposed to dry or moist air it is unalterable and does not oxidize or tarnish like most of the common metals. Neither cold nor hot water has any action on it. It is not affected by sulfureted hydrogen, the gas that so easily tarnishes silver.

Hard as iron

"It preserves its appearance under all ordinary circumstances as perfectly as gold. It is a soft metal like pure silver, but when rolled or compressed it becomes as hard as iron. It has only one-fourth the weight of silver and less than one-third the weight of copper.

"A metal with so many advantages should be used for all coins made of copper or bronze. It is not so much the value of the material or metal used in minor coins as the adaptability and convenience.

"The change of the minor coins to aluminum would increase the number of collectors as all changes in coinage create interest in and observation of coins. As a natural consequence it would be to the interest of collectors . . . to have this desirable change in metal made."

However, Wismer's plea was ignored. The U.S. Mint was not ready to issue aluminum coins—certainly not for the sake of boosting interest in numismatics! Collectors would have to look abroad for the first circulation strike aluminum coins.

Empowered by an Order of Council that was approved June 30, 1906, the London Royal Mint struck aluminum one-tenth penny pieces for the Protectorate of Nigeria in 1906 and 1907. It also struck 900,000 aluminum half cents and 6.9 million aluminum cents for

Uganda in 1907.

Previously, cowry shells, which fluctuated in value, had served as money in the interior regions of Africa. "It is hoped that these small aluminum coins will gradually take their place as the medium of exchange," said Deputy Master of the Mint Ellison McCartney. "They have a fixed value, which ought to be a great advantage to the native as well as the general trade of the country."

The new coins were holed in the center to permit the natives to string them together, as had been their habit with the cowries from time immemorial.

The greater the cost

The low face value of the coins and the immense number that were required made it necessary to strike them in an extremely light metal. "The smaller the amount, the greater the cost of coinage," McCartney explained. "Half pence are much more costly to coin than pennies, and yield far less profit." He added, "So far as I know, these are the only aluminum coins in the world."

In 1908 the Royal Mint struck more than 8.3 million aluminum cents for Nigeria, including a small quantity of Proofs for collectors. However, the aluminum coins soon proved to be unsuited to the tropical climate, which hastened corrosion. Copper-nickel coins of smaller size were substituted for the aluminum pieces in the latter part of the year.

Despite disappointment with regard to the first circulating aluminum coins, interest in aluminum coinage remained strong. In 1909, a fascinating item appeared in *The Numismatist*:

"It has been proposed in France to adopt aluminum for the pieces of 10 and 5 centimes, which are now made of bronze. The advantage urged are the durability of the metal, its malleability, its metallic sonority and its lightness.

"Great stress is laid on this last point, which, it is asserted, would enable the small coins to be easily distinguished from silver in the pocket and make it possible to carry them in quantity without being annoyed by the weight.

"The Paris Mint has already struck a number of 5- and 10-centime pieces of the new metal, and their production is said to be as easy as the striking of copper pieces. The same dies were used as for the copper coins, and the new aluminum ones . . . will be exactly the same size, thickness, and design as the old coppers. Of course, they will be very much lighter and will look neater and cleaner. The reign of aluminum may, therefore, begin any moment."

This prediction was somewhat premature; circulating aluminum coins were still a thing of the future in France. In 1914, however, a private firm in Denver turned out aluminum one-centavo pieces for the state of Durango, Mexico.

Germany, facing copper shortages brought on by World War I, struck aluminum one-pfennig pieces in 1918. The German Republic went on to strike a succession of aluminum coins in the postwar years: 50-pfennig pieces in 1922 and 1935; a pair of 3-mark pieces in 1922 (one of which celebrated the Weimar Constitution); and 200- and 500-mark pieces in 1923.

Romania and Greece

In 1921, Romania issued 25- and 50-bani aluminum coins, and in 1922 Greece minted a 10-lepta aluminum coin. Bulgaria struck 1- and 2-leva aluminum pieces in 1923. In 1938 Paraguay struck 50-centavos, one-peso and two-peso coins in aluminum. Japan adopted aluminum for coinage the same year.

World War II needs brought tremendous growth in the aluminum industry, and production shot to record levels. Aluminum was especially valued as a substitute for metals that were required for the war effort. Nickel, for example, formed an important part of armor plate, while huge quantities of copper were used for motors, generators, transformers, wiring, ignition systems, radio receivers, radar instruments and shell cases.

Vitally important airplanes

China, France, Germany and Japan were among the nations which struck aluminum coins during the war. In the United States and England, however, aluminum was needed for vitally important airplanes and lightweight parts, so other solutions to the coinage problem had to be found.

In the mid-1970s rising copper prices prompted the U.S. Mint to again take a closer look at aluminum. A number of pattern aluminum cents were struck in 1974, some of which were never returned by members of a congressional committee. Kenneth E. Bressett, editor of *A Guide Book of United States Coins,* estimates that six specimens may exist.

On a legal basis, at least, the aluminum cent failed to materialize.

The Numismatist's Topside Companion

Today a simple fact remains—the United States, a pioneer in aluminum coin experimentation, has yet to issue its first circulating aluminum coin.

Coin Market Cycles

| by Q. David Bowers | 1993 |

The following was written for the "Coins and Collectors" column in The Numismatist, 1993.

I have always liked the study of economics. Perhaps it is because economic theories are subject to change, and the entire field is somewhat of a black art. I first encountered economics in a serious way when I was a student at Penn State in the late 1950s. I was particularly fascinated by business cycles, ranging from the Building Cycle (based upon construction) to the 50-year Kondratieff Cycle, and more, plus numerous other ups and downs which weren't known at that time. Since then the computer age has descended upon us, and even more cycles have been identified.

Some cycles are like Halley's Comet; they are sharp and recognizable in one era, and then fade away to inconsequence in another.

Despite its billions of dollars in resources, and unlimited access to academic, financial, and other expertise, the United States government does not have the foggiest idea as to whether interest rates will be a point higher a year from now, or a point lower; nor does anyone know whether gold six months from now will be up $25 per ounce, the same, or down $25 per ounce, or what retail sales of consumer goods will be, or what unemployment figures will show, or answers to a host of other important indications.

Many years ago I chanced upon a copy of a book written in the

1840s by Charles MacKay, titled *Extraordinary Popular Delusions and the Madness of Crowds.* My attention had been called to this by reading the biography of financier Bernard Baruch, who credited this volume with much of the success he had in buying and selling stocks at the right time. I was reminded of the MacKay book recently, and thought about writing about the topic of this column when I parted with $16 to acquire a copy of a current book, *A Short History of Financial Euphoria,* by John Kenneth Galbraith, distinguished writer in finance and economics. As have many other writers over the years, Galbraith drew upon MacKay's 1841 study, noting in the credits: "While superseded in some matters by later research and writing, it remains today one of the most engaging and colorful accounts of speculative aberrations."

Perhaps it was only natural in the 1950s—when I first read the MacKay book—that I attempted to transfer some of this knowledge to numismatics. The first coin market "crash" I personally witnessed occurred in 1957. While not exactly having all of the earmarks of the Dutch tulip bulb mania delineated by McKay, the rage for current Proof sets did have many similarities—including a disregard for facts, an overlooking of true demand, and a blind belief that, somehow, no matter what the price paid was, someone would come along and pay more later (now popularly called the "greater fool theory").

I sensed that something was going wrong with Proof set prices, and with my friend Jim Ruddy (who was to become my business partner the next year, 1958) I liquidated right before the market break a holding of Proof sets I had acquired.

In the early 1960s I decided to study coin market cycles in earnest and in 1962 published the first study ever on the field which appeared in *The Empire Investors' Report.* By going through back issues of *The Numismatist's* old auction catalogues, copies of the *American Journal of Numismatics,* reference books, and other sources, I was able to document quite a few market peaks and breaks. A discussion of these later appeared in my book, *High Profits in Rare Coin Investment* (first edition published in 1974, followed by 12 later editions).

One of the earliest peaks I documented was in Washington tokens and medals, which increased greatly in price circa 1860, when the largest of all "coin dealers" at the time, the Philadelphia Mint, was eagerly buying and trading specimens for its Washington cabinet, even going so far as to restrike rarities in order to acquire pieces it needed. The Mint's buying campaign culminated on February 22, 1860, with the dedication of a marvelous display of Washington pieces at the Mint. However, market interest went beyond that point, and collector enthusiasm remained strong for several years thereafter. By the late 1860s, interest had faded, with the result that decades passed, and still some of the price records of the mid-1860s were not attained.

After a while, market cycles became very well defined in my eyes. I found that certain coin series responded differently than others. In other words, silver dollars may be going up in price while pattern coins are going down, or gold coins may be falling while the values of colonial pieces are on the rise.

Many, if not most, coin market cycles have been based upon cause and effect considerations, rather than regularly spaced intervals on the calendar. Thus, in the late 19th century, and continuing for the first few years of the 1900s, there was a spate of interest in Hard Times tokens privately issued, circa 1832-1844, due to the publication of Lyman H. Low's book (titled, appropriately enough, *Hard Times Tokens*) on the subject, the enthusiasm spread by Benjamin Wright, M.D. (a token specialist who wrote articles for *The Numismatist,* and served as president of the American Numismatic Association), and the availability of pieces in dealers' stocks.

From about 1910 to about 1940, Hard Times tokens and other early tokens were, in effect, dead. Then came several market stimuli. Wayte Raymond listed early tokens in his *Standard Catalogue of U.S. Coins,* the most-used arbiter of coin values. Later, the father-and-son team of Melvin and George Fuld instituted a monthly column on tokens in *The Numismatist.* In 1955, Charles V. Kappen reissued Low's turn-of-the-century *Hard Times Tokens* book. A few years later, the Token and Medal Society (TAMS) was founded. In the 1980s, with updates since then, Russell Rulau published several price guides to tokens.

The market cycles for Hard Times tokens have been primarily defined by collectors, rather than investors. Many other market cycles, in fact most in recent decades, have been influenced by coin investment. The wide availability of pricing data, plus publicity given to the advantages of investment, have brought many buyers into the field. Coin market cycles based upon investment have included these areas during the past 50 years:

▼ Commemoratives, especially half dollars
▼ Rolls and Proof sets
▼ 19th and early 20th century Proof coins
▼ Gold coins
▼ MS-65 and Proof-65 (and finer) certified coins

An example of the latter cycle peak is provided by an 1878-CC trade dollar in MS-65 grade which had a *Coin World* "Trends" value of $150,000 at the height of the coin investment market a few years ago, but which now lists for $27,000—same coin, same grade, but a different price.

Coin booms and busts have certain well-defined characteristics. To reiterate, in recent booms and busts the public has become interested in coins in a big way, not because of any numismatic or historical appeal they may have, but on price alone. Because of this, relatively little attention is paid to studying coins, no effort is made to join numismatic organizations, and the object is, as Walter Breen might say if he were living today (at least he said it in the past concerning certain coins), G-R-E-E-D. Coin dealers, including many new ones who are attracted to what is going on, help the rise by extolling the investment potential of coins, sometimes promising high returns, but having little knowledge to back up the promises.

In general, the pieces that go up the fastest attract the most attention. Tremendous amounts of "new money" come into the market, scaring collectors away. Soon, the particular segment of the market participating in the boom is left almost entirely to investors—collectors are no longer interested because the prices are too high. Readers may recall that this is precisely what happened with MS-65 and finer and Proof-65 and finer coins in the late 1980s, culminating in a market peak in March 1989.

Once the supply of "fresh money" ends—as it always does at some point—the market collapses; simply because there is not basic or fundamental demand from numismatists, at least not at anything near the high levels just attained. Eventually, the market drops downward to the point at which numismatists once again take part. At this point, numismatists have the fortunate aspect of buying at or near the low point of the market cycle, for this is when the values seem to be the greatest. In the meantime, when the market is at a low cycle, investors are scarce—as indeed they are today in 1993—so they do not have much competition. Collectors gather collections, and make many excellent buys in doing so.

Sooner or later, investment rears its head once again, more "new money" comes into the market, and some area of the market (the area seems to differ from one market boom to another) will feel the effects and rise beyond the prices any *collector* wishes to pay. Wise collectors will sell or auction their coins and cash in at, or near, the crest. At the very least, they will stop buying the particular series in demand, and turn their attention elsewhere.

What can be learned from this commentary? In a nutshell, if the coins in a given series seem to be increasing in value very quickly and are not basically rare, and if the main sales appeal for the coins seems to be investment potential (rather than numismatic desirability), be careful!

The entire cyclical situation is like the tortoise and the hare—with dedicated numismatists being the tortoises, and the investors being the hares.

Action at the Local Level

by Q. David Bowers   1993

The following was written for "The Joys of Collecting" column in COIN WORLD, *1993.*

When I attend coin conventions, I usually go with checkbook in hand, to buy for inventory and my clients' needs. Of course, there are other things to do—such as selling coins and saying "hello" to old and new friends—but buying is typically my number one consideration. Nice coins sell themselves, but buying them is an effort.

At a large show last year, I wanted to buy some nice Extremely Fine, AU, and MS-60 Indian cents, not only of scarce dates such as those in the early 1870s, but of common issues as well. I encountered a problem. While I saw many gorgeous high-level Mint State and Proof coins certified by PCGS and others, and bought quite a few, during the course of the convention I simply could not find the commoner dates in lower grades! Similarly, if I wanted to buy a 1915 Panama Pacific set for the best part of $100,000, I would have had several opportunities. But, a want list for inexpensive Barber half dollars 1892-1915 in AU grade went largely unfilled.

"What's wrong with this picture?"—as cartoons in the Sunday paper sometimes ask.

The answer is that while advanced collectors had many opportunities to spend thousands of dollars, a beginner would have had little from which to select. In fact, in one dealer's showcase the cheapest coin was

$15,000! As you might suspect, I am leading up to something.

The other day I noticed a mention in a collectors' magazine that an old bottle show would be held at the High School in Kennebunk, Maine, on Sunday, April 4th. I sent for information.

By return mail came a two-page *personal* letter and a printed flyer from the organizer, Dallas Willbanks. Almost apologetically, he said, "We are a medium-size show, averaging about 75 to 80 tables each of the past five years." Further: "The show has always had a good cross-section of items for sale. The show attracts dealers and buyers from all over New England as well as New York and New Jersey."

I collect bottles casually. For me, a typical purchase is in the $10 to $100 range. Some of them are coin-related, such as Ayer's Sarsaparilla and Drake's Plantation Bitters, produced by firms that also issued encased postage stamps.

Reflecting on numismatics for a moment, I could not help but wonder how great the growth would be in our hobby if we had lots of "little" local and regional coin shows with the enthusiasm of this one!

The Copper Company of Upper Canada

by John J. Ford, Jr.   RCR 65 1987

The following article originally appeared in The Coin Collector's Journal, *May-June 1951, and was called to our attention by John J. Ford, Jr., the author, when he read our description of Lot 3078 in our Taylor Collection Sale (March 1987). The Taylor specimen of the Copper Company of Upper Canada was listed with the statement that it "probably dates from circa 1805 to 1810." At the sale itself this was corrected, the attention of bidders was called to its nature as a piece made in later years, and it sold for $357.50.*

The limited interest in the earlier issues of our country, together with those of our neighbor to the north, by the present generation of collectors, seems to stem from a decided lack of exposure to the fascinating background often connected with such pieces.

Almost 80 years ago, Thomas Wilson, the avid pioneer collector of Canadian coins, introduced one of the first specimens of the Copper Company of Upper Canada tokens to the collecting gentry of North America. The obverse of the piece portrayed a reclining river god holding a trident aloft and the date, 1794, below. The legend FERTILITATEM DIVITIAS QUE CIRCUMFERREMUS, displayed in incused letters about the circumference of the coin, was freely translated as "Distributing Fertility and Wealth." The name of the engraver, PONTHON, also appeared upon the obverse of the piece. The reverse was comparatively simple, COPPER COMPANY OF UPPER

CANADA within a circle, surrounded by the denomination, ONE HALF PENNY.

In 1869, immediately prior to Mr. Wilson's acquisition of his specimen, Alfred Sandham, in his *Coins Tokens and Medals of the Dominion of Canada,* quoted a description by the Rev. Christmas Sandham, observed that "This coin was struck in England for the Company, and cannot have been very extensively circulated, from the fact that, as far as we are aware, no cabinet in Canada possesses a specimen." (Sandham, p.7; p.21, No.4; Pl-l, No. 9).

After Sandham's attempt at fanning to flame a growing interest in Canadian numismatics, a number of other authors succeeded in describing a large number of early Canadian items. Almost all of these made mention of the Copper Company of Upper Canada token.

Dr. Joseph LeRoux, in 1882, published a *Complete Canadian Copper Coin Catalog.* In it, he listed the Copper Company piece as No. 47 and mentioned that he desired the coin for his personal collection. The following year, LeRoux again listed the piece, this time in his *Numismatic Atlas for Canada.* Here, he illustrated the coin (P-6) and indicated its rarity as excessive (No. 64, Rarity-7), mentioning that the piece had already sold for $15. In 1888 and 1892, Dr. LeRoux published the first and second editions of his famous *Canadian Coin Cabinet,* and, both instances, advanced the rarity of the Copper Company coins to Rarity-8 which meant the item was "precious." (LeRoux, P-122, No. 696.)

The LeRoux works undoubtedly inspired P. Napoleon Breton of Montreal who, in 1890, published a small pamphlet on Canadian material which was extremely popular and ran to 5,000 copies in two editions. Breton, in 1894, published his famous and momentous work, *The History of the Coins and Tokens Relating to Canada.* In this standard reference, Breton listed the Copper Company of Upper Canada token as No. 721 and rated it as Rarity-5. (Worth from $50 to $100). In spite of this relatively high valuation, Breton condemned the piece in the text. "This is the first coin struck for Canada after the conquest. As all known specimens of this piece are Proofs, we may conclude that it was never issued for circulation, and that the dies are probably in the hands of some collector who issues specimens from time to time so as not to break the price."

Breton's book inspired the collecting of Canadian coins and tokens to its greatest height and such famous collectors as McLachlan,

The Copper Company of Upper Canada

Michaud, the Harts, Campeau, Casault, Boucher, and others, often paid high prices for such rarities as the Copper Company piece. This tremendous interest and demand, inspired by well-to-do collectors and influenced by keen students, soon became the inspiration for operations of a very odd nature.

The Muling

The Copper Company of Upper Canada halfpenny reverse had long been known muled with the reverse of the famous 1796 Myddleton (Kentucky) token (Breton, P-117, No. 722). The first recorded specimen of the mule, on this side of the Atlantic, appeared a very few years prior to the introduction of the regular type. The Mickley Collection, sold in New York in 1867, possessed a specimen of the muling which served as a basis for the illustration in Sandham's book. Sandham's mention of the mule was followed by LeRoux, who, in his 1883, 1888, and 1892 publications, listed the item as slightly less rare than the regular Copper Company piece. (LeRoux, 1883. No. 65, Rarity-6, Sales record of $13; 1888 to 1892 No. 697, Rarity-7—extremely rare).

The odd fabric of the muling perhaps influenced general opinion of the regular piece. In 1886, Robert W. McLachlan, perhaps the greatest Canadian numismatist, penned a small booklet called *A Descriptive Catalog of Coins, Tokens & Medals*. McLachlan listed both the regular variety and the mule, and his comments concerning each are of great interest. He listed the Copper Company variety as No. CCXIX and rated it as Rarity-6. "This is the earliest coin struck for Canada subsequent to the conquest. The execution of the piece is of a high order, similar to the better class of the 18th-century tokens. There seems never to have been any issue of this token for circulation, as no specimen has ever been met with here in change, nor do any of the older collectors include an impression among their lists of rarities. The only known examples are Proofs that have come from some English numismatist." The mule was listed as No. CCXX and also rated as Rarity-6. "This, like the former one, is rare, never having gone into general circulation; they both are really English trade tokens of the 18th-century, and are no doubt from the hands of the same engraver, as are the one-penny and one-cent pieces of Sierra Leone, to which they bear a close resemblance. Proofs of these latter coins are sold at from one to two shillings in London, while the Copper Company pieces bring from $15 to $20. If the dies are still in existence, as the fact that these Proof mule pieces turn up so regularly would seem to indicate, they have been carefully manipulated to keep up the price so well." (See also the *American Journal of Numismatics,* Vol. XVI, page 34.)

McLachlan's caustic appraisal of the muling and his concern regarding the possible misuse of the dies presumably influenced Breton in his opinion of both varieties.

While actually, Mr. M.'s feelings in the matter were only faintly correct in the case of the muling and completely wrong regarding the regular Copper Company piece, both he and P.N. Breton unknowingly anticipated the realization of their worst fears.

Thus, at a time when the origin of the regular Copper Company variety was shrouded in mystery and the repetitious appearance, together with the general make-up of the muling, was seriously open to question, many collectors in the British Isles, Canada and the United States received a very interesting communication.

The J.R. Thomas Card and Order Form

In the late Spring of 1894, one J. Rochelle Thomas, a dealer in coins and medals located in London, contacted many prominent collectors via a small card or circular. Mr. Thomas stated that the "Original dies" of the rare halfpenny of the Copper Company of Upper Canada had recently been discovered and that they were currently in his possession. In an obvious effort to capitalize upon the limited number of regular Copper Company pieces known, Mr. Thomas offered Proof impressions from his dies at 42 shillings in silver and at 21 shillings in bronze. This offer was substantiated, on the same card, by the announcement that only 12 pieces were struck in silver and but 50 in bronze. Thomas was undoubtedly an early and enthusiastic adherent of the direct mail type of advertising as his card included a small order form which could be easily detached.

The Thomas "Numismatist" Ad

The May 1894 issue of *The Numismatist* carried an advertisement by J.R. Thomas which closely resembled the card he had sent through the mails. In his ad, Thomas priced his wares in dollars; the silver piece at $10 and the bronze at $5. As both illustrations prove, J.R.T. maintained his contention that he had the original dies.

The prevalent belief that Thomas did have the original dies and that he was, more or less, pandering the value of the original coins, caused Dr. Marvin to publish an article in *The American Journal of Numismatics* commenting rather severely upon the reprehensible practice of resurrecting old dies and producing restrikes from them. The temper of the Marvin article was based upon the sale of these coins, by Thomas, at a figure which was quite moderate when compared with the value of the originals, to people who considered them almost as desirable. As the A.J.N. article is of considerable importance, we reprint it here as it originally appeared in the A.J.N., Vol. XXXIX, No. 1, Page 19 July 1894).

Recent Restrike of a Canadian Token

We learn that the dies of the halfpenny token of the Copper Company of Upper Canada have recently been discovered in England, and it is with the utmost dissatisfaction that we have read an announcement of a dealer in that country, that they are now in his possession, and that he will strike 12 specimens in silver and 50 in bronze, at $10 and $5 respectively.

It is by such mercenary and much to be deplored proceedings as this, that the science is smirched, and suspicion unjustly cast upon it. It is detrimental to both the collector and the dealer. There are far too many pieces of this class circulating from cabinet to cabinet, and frequently through the medium of the auction room. It is true their character is sometimes plainly indicated, but they are often smuggled into the market without a word of comment, or described in terms purposely misleading. We are of the opinion that all those who value and esteem the science and desire to see its integrity and authenticity preserved, will carefully withhold their countenance from the proposed enterprise of Mr. J. Rochelle Thomas, and decline to purchase his "Brummagem" wares.

It is high time that a vigorous crusade was inaugurated against all manner of imitations, as well as those who exploit them; and complaisant dealers who accommodate owners by foisting their spurious pieces upon the market, should be promptly and determinedly frowned down. Surely the genuine and bona fide field is large enough to afford a profitable scope for reputable dealers.

The October 1894 number of Spink's *Numismatic Circular,* the house organ of the highly respected British dealers, copied the Marvin article as it originally appeared, and, according to R.W. McLachlan, for this indiscretion had to pay a considerable amount of damages.

In any event, Spink apologized to Mr. Thomas in the April 1895 number of their magazine. Their apology fits in well with our story and therefore we reproduce it here.

Recent Restrike of Canadian Token

In our issue of October 1894 we reproduced an article which appeared in the *American Journal of Numismatics* for the previous July on the above subject; which Mr. J. Rochelle Thomas considered cast serious reflections upon his character and business, and he thereupon commenced an action against us which has now been happily arranged on terms satisfactory to him.

We desire by this to apologize to him for any seeming reflections by the article and unreservedly withdraw such statements, and regret that the same was reproduced by us. In such reproduction we were not imbued with the least feeling against Mr. Thomas, with whom for many years we have had considerable business transactions and by the insertion of the article complained of our only desire was to further the interest of the numismatic art generally and not exceed the bounds of fair criticism.

At the same time the British firm reprinted the *A.J.N.* article and thereby raised the ire of Mr. Thomas, R.W. McLachlan wrote to the *American Journal of Numismatics* concerning the so-called restrikes and called attention to the prophetic attributes of his earlier writings. On page 62 of the October 1894 *Journal,* McLachlan's letter is reproduced in full.

Mr. McLachlan's observations, at this point, seem somewhat ambiguous. It appears obvious that he was not fully familiar, at that time, with the nature of the Thomas productions. He cautioned the purchasers of the "restrikes" not to confuse them with the pieces previously sold. In the same breath, McLachlan went on to state that the issues which have occasionally appeared during the past few years were possibly themselves merely restrikes.

The renowned Canadian numismatist undoubtedly shared the popular belief that the Thomas pieces were identical with the originals struck a century earlier. This belief probably substantiated his earlier theories concerning the possible existence of the dies and the annual manufacture of specimens. The truth of the matter is that Thomas did not have the original dies at all. His were either contemporary dies cut at the same time as those used to strike the original coins, or as is more likely, were out and out frauds. Mr. McLachlan, in an address read at the 1912 *ANA* Rochester convention, corrected many of of his earlier

The Copper Company of Upper Canada

ideas concerning the Copper Company pieces and stated that the Thomas specimens were forgeries. "And yet a comparison of the original, with the so-called restrike, clearly shows the latter to be a clever forgery, for while at an ordinary glance, no difference is noticeable, so close is the imitation, both obverse and reverse dies differ in many minor details. One of these differences can easily be noted. The Rs in "COPPER" and "UPPER," which in the genuine are old style with straight ends, in the false are new style with curved ends."

The reverses of the original Copper Company piece and the Thomas impression, when compared, leave little doubt as to the variance in fabrication. We have always used the "O" in COPPER as a criterion; the letter in the original being perfectly round, while in the forgery, the letter is decidedly oval in shape.

Modern writers on the subject of the Copper Company pieces seem more than a little confused. Mr. Howard Kurth, an excellent and unusally methodical student, presented, some years ago, a paper to the Albany Numismatic Society titled "Canadian Coppers." This article later appeared in the *Numismatic Scrapbook Magazine*. In it, Mr. Kurth questioned the origin of the Copper Company pieces and evidently was not familiar with the history of the so-called restrikes. We quote from his article:

One of the earliest tokens referring to Canada is the rare halfpenny of 1794 inscribed, "Copper Company of Upper Canada" (B-721). This beautiful token, showing on the obverse a reclining river god, was never intended for circulation. It is believed to have been fabricated by some coin dealer in England especially to be sold to collectors. The few examples known are all in perfect condition. A die variety having an oval-shaped "O" in the word "Copper" is thought to be a later copy, and is less rare than the so-called original, but why it should be considered any less authentic is not quite clear. Another rarity (B-722) was synthesized by muling the "Copper Company" die with the reverse of the Myddelton "Kentucky" token of 1796.

Another noted numismatist and good friend of ours, Mr. J. Douglas Ferguson, wrote concerning the Copper Company of Upper Canada pieces in his "Canadian Coin Notes" which appeared in this *Journal* nearly 11 years ago. Mr. Ferguson quoted Mr. McLachlan's famous article on the "Copper Tokens of Upper Canada" which appeared in the 1915 *A.J.N.* At the time, McLachlan seemed to rest content with the theory that while referring to the coin as being the earliest relating to the province, struck under British rule, it is in reality an English 18th-century trade token, issued, as he believed, as a speculation by some English coin dealer for sale to collectors.

This is not the case. The Copper Company of Upper Canada halfpenny is, in fact, a definite pattern for an authentic Canadian copper coinage. The full story is told by Paul Montgomery in his *The Romance of Canada's Money* published in 1933.

The Constitutional Act of 1791 effected a great political change in Canada by dividing the province into Upper and Lower Canada. The next year, General John Graves Simcoe was appointed governor of Upper Canada. Earlier in 1787, a law was passed by the British Parliament which prohibited the importation and circulation of "any halfpence or other copper coin, other than Tower halfpence or such copper as may and do legally pass current in Great Britain and Ireland." For a great many reasons, this act did not prove a solution to the currency problems that troubled Canada and, in fact, had a contrary effect for it tended to denude the country of all copper coinage. Shortly after Gov. Simcoe took office, the first parliamentary gathering was held at Newark (now Niagara on the Lake). Many valuable details of this meeting, together with records of other early legislation, were lost due to their destruction by fire in 1813. It is known however, that Gov. Simcoe gave serious consideration to the state of money, or the lack of it, then in circulation in his domain. After numerous debates upon the subject, it was decided that it would be very advantageous to have a distinctive coinage for Upper Canada. A committee was appointed to consider the matter of design, minting, and any pertinent suggestions brought to their attention concerning the proposed new coin.

An order was placed with the highly regarded firm of Boulton and Watt, and the pieces were struck at their establishment at Staffordshire, near Birmingham. The dies were cut by Ponthon, a British diesinker of the period who was then employed at the Soho Mint. Ponthon was an unusually skilled diecutter who designed and engraved a number of dies including those for the Daniel Eccleston, Lancaster halfpenny.

The patterns were shipped to Canada and late in 1794 were exhibited to the legislature. Gov. Simcoe, having gone this far with the experiment, thought it advisable to take the Home Office into his confidence. Accordingly, samples of the Copper Company of Upper Canada pieces were sent back to England with a request for permission to circulate them. Simcoe's letter reviewed the poor monetary situation in the colony and vividly described the obstacles facing any serious efforts towards serious trade expansion. The home government refused to grant permission for active manufacture and circulation of the halfpennies, but were not unsympathetic toward the governor's plea for monetary reform. Instead of permitting the beautiful coins by Boulton and Watt to be manufactured and circulated, a shipment of worn and poor coppers was sent to Canada from Ireland. This "junk" was replaced in Ireland by a new issue of pieces made expressly for circulation there, as it was believed the North American colony would be satisfied with the nondescript material removed from Irish circulation.

The Copper Company inscription on the patterns seems to be based upon early exploitation of the copper mines to the north of lakes Superior and Huron. Perhaps the basic plan was to manufacture coins abroad from native Canadian copper, but we will probably never know due to the unfortunate loss of the records.

To further strengthen the background of the Copper Company pattern, reference can be made to *The Nineteenth Century Token Coinage* by W.J. Davis, 1904. On page XIX, Davis lists coins and medals struck at the Soho Mint, Staffordshire, by Boulton and Watt. This account is taken from an early circular letter printed by that firm and listing their most attractive productions in an evident attempt to obtain new customers. Under colonial, miscellaneous, we find the Copper Company of Upper Canada halfpenny.

It is extremely odd that the Myddelton tokens or the Myddleton (British Settlement Kentucky) Copper Company mule cannot be found in the early Boulton and Watt list. The Myddelton pieces have long been considered an American colonial issue and we firmly believe that they were made for an Anglo-American colonization society somewhat on the order of the French Castorland situation. While we can only assume and attempt to place the threads together, it must be remembered that either French or British colonization, particularly the latter, would have been a very touchy political proposition during that period, up to and including the time that the Boulton and Watt list was circulated.

The Numismatist's Topside Companion

The Myddelton Company mule, combining the two reverses, was undoubtedly made during the craze for tokens which prevailed in England, 1794 to 1797, or even a few years thereafter. It was perhaps, a production of Young, Till, and Taylor, the two former dealers in coins and medals, who, according to Davis, muled Boulton's dies somewhat extensively (Davis, P-XVII).

According to L. Forrer in his *Biographical Dictionary of Medallists*, Ponthon cut the dies for both the regular Copper Company issue and the muling. On the other hand, a coin described as a pattern for a Kentucky coin, in silver, presumably a Myddelton, dated 1796, appeared in a Sotheby sale in March 1819 in London. The piece described was said to be by KNUCKLER. This could only have been Conrad H. Kuchler, a German medallist and coin engraver employed at Soho, 1790 through 1806. We differ with Forrer, and believe that the Myddelton tokens, both obverse and reverse dies, were cut by Kuchler and that the mule represents a hybrid product, the fruit of two engravers.

The original Copper Company piece as well as examples of the Myddelton token in both metals can be found on page No. 246 of the *Provincial Copper Coins, Tokens, Tickets and Medalets issued in Great Britain, Ireland, and the Colonies* by Thomas Sharp, London, 1834. Other early listings and records indicate that the Copper Company pattern and the Myddelton patterns, if the latter can be called such, are strictly contemporary pieces. The mule is probably an authentic restrike manufactured at an early date solely for the collecting fraternity. We differ with McLachlan in that we believe the mules could have all been made at an early period and the dies destroyed or lost. The steady appearance of the mulings during the last part of the 19th century was undoubtedly the result of careful handling and dispersion of a small hoard of such pieces.

A detailed listing of the Copper Company of Upper Canada patterns and forgeries and the Myddelton (British Settlement Kentucky) Copper Company mules is presented herewith to remove all possibility of confusion. The valuations given are based upon a careful study of all available records, particularly the appearance of various specimens at public sale during the past 75 years.

1794 PATTERN. Obv. River God. FERTILITATEM DIVITIAS QUE CIRCUMFERREMUS. Ponthon. Rev. COPPER COMPANY OF

The Copper Company of Upper Canada

UPPER CANADA within circle. Around ONE HALF PENNY.
Breton-721. Raymond-71. Bronze. (Proofs only) $75.
A specimen of the original is known in pewter or lead. Impressions are also known of the obverse only, one struck before the legends were added, in the same composition. See the J.G. Murdoch sale, 1903.

1794 FORGERY. As above. Struck by Thomas. (1894)
Breton-721. Raymond-72. Bronze. (Also with a bronzed surface) (Proofs only) $5
Raymond-72a. White metal. (resembles tin) $7.50
Raymond-72b. Silver $17.50
Specimens are also known in gold and in lead. See Murdoch and W.W.C. Wilson sales.

1796 MULING. Obv. Hope presenting a male and female child to America. BRITISH SETTLEMENT KENTUCKY. Rev. COPPER COMPANY OF UPPER CANADA within circle. Around, ONE HALF PENNY.
Breton-722. Raymond-73. Bronze (Proofs only) $60
Several authorities, including Atkins and Breton (1912) insist the mule is known in silver. We have never seen a specimen.

Did You Know?

| from Rare Coin Review No. 92 | 1993 |

▼ **The 1936-D Washington quarter** is rare in Uncirculated grade not because the mintage is low, which is isn't, but because collectors were preoccupied with other things—such as commemoratives—and forgot to save them!

▼ **Is it Nolan Ryan** who is depicted on the 1992 Olympic commemorative silver dollar? The designer says it is a composite. However, on April 2, 1992, when ANA President Ed Rochette was at the store in the lobby of the U.S. Mint in Philadelphia, he asked the clerk for a "Nolan Ryan dollar" and the lady on duty promptly handed him a 1992 Olympic commemorative!

▼ **All 1858/7 overdate Flying Eagle cents** have the eagle's wing tip toward the top of the coin broken at the end. Even if you can't see the overdate clearly, this is a quick way to tell the variety. Of course, if you are paying for an overdate, it's nice to be able to see the overdate, too.

▼ **Until 1836,** all coins at the Philadelphia Mint were struck with manpower—men swung weighted levers which actuated screw presses. Meanwhile in England, technology was more advanced, and Boulton & Watt had perfected a high-speed, automatically fed coining press by the 1790s.

▼ **The only Sherlock Holmes** mystery story featuring a numismatist is "The Adventure of the Three Garridebs."—interesting reading, and available in just about any Holmes anthology.

▼ **Even worn Eisenhower** dollars now have a premium value and sell for $1.20 or so, according to an interesting article in a recent issue of Numismatic News. I guess the Federal Reserve has run out of them, and they are now collectors' items. In the meantime, hundreds of millions of Susan B. Anthony dollars are still available at face value.

▼ **Odd anniversary:** In 1991 we had a commemorative silver dollar observing the 38th anniversary of the end of the Korean War, and in 1993 we have another commemorative dollar marking the 202nd anniversary of the Bill of Rights. What the Mint needs to do to increase sales—witness what happened to the postage stamp recently—is put out a commemorative depicting Elvis. Now that we don't have to make anniversaries come out even, such as the 50th or 100th, we can observe the 58th anniversary of Elvis' birth, or anything else in his life. In the 1970s, when Elvis was playing in Las Vegas, a friend of our company invited the entire staff to be his guests at the Hilton International, where we enjoyed several days of being wined and dined, seeing Elvis, and talking with Col. Tom Parker—not exactly numismatic, of course, but very memorable.

▼ **In 1873** a dollar was coined in three distinctly different forms: the Liberty Seated silver dollar, the silver trade dollar, and the gold dollar.

▼ **1941 Proof Liberty Walking half dollars** exist with and without the monogram AW of the designer, Adolph Weinman, on the reverse. Many impressions were struck with the initials removed by polishing. However, the different varieties have attracted relatively little attention, and most numismatists are content with just one example of the date.

▼ **Certain 1836 and 1839 Gobrecht dollars** are regular issues, not patterns, and should be collected as such. Included are 1,600 strikings of the 1836 with starless obverse, starry reverse, and plain edge, and 300 1839 Gobrecht dollars with starry obverse, starless reverse, and reeded edge.

▼ **R.S. ("Dick") Yeoman,** long-time editor of the Guide Book, told a story in which at a convention a collector approached him and said, "I have a Guide Book that has been bound upside down." Always eager to please, Dick Yeoman said, "I'm sorry to hear that. I would be happy to replace it with a perfect copy," whereupon the collector replied something to the effect of "Are you kidding? I have been offered $200 for it!"

▼ **1883 Hawaiian silver coins** were struck at the San Francisco

Did You Know?

Mint, but without a mintmark. At the time Hawaii was an independent island kingdom.

▼ **1925 Vancouver commemorative** half dollars were struck at the San Francisco Mint, but without a mintmark. Why? No one knows. Apparently, they forgot to put a mintmark on the die.

▼ **The world's largest "coin dealer"** is the U.S. Mint. During the past decade it has sold far more coins than any other entity, has employed more people, and has spent more on advertising.

▼ **Commemorative half dollars** can be collected by state or region. For example, if you live in Connecticut there is the 1935 Connecticut Tercentenary issue and the 1936 Bridgeport. Peruse the pages of the *Guide Book* and see how many commemoratives you can find from your state or general geographical area.

Reminiscences of Julius Guttag by His Son

by Alvin Guttag

The following reminiscences are from the pen of Alvin Guttag, son of Julius Guttag, one of the principals of the Guttag Brothers, prominent numismatists of the 1920s and early 1930s:

My father, Julius Guttag, was born on November 1, 1884 and died on March 27, 1962, shortly before the birth of his fifth grandchild, Mark Julius Guttag. He was a very devoted family man and proud of any achievements of his children and grandchildren. Next to his family, his first love was coins.

He had three children; two, Erma and Alvin, with his first wife and one; Evelyn, with his second wife. His first wife died in the influenza epidemic of 1918. Like Theodore Roosevelt, to the best of my knowledge, he never mentioned her again. However, he helped to take care of her mother (who was a widow) for many years until her death. Also he made sure that she was included in many family gatherings.

(When I refer to my "mother" in the remainder of this article it is to my stepmother, who is the only mother I ever knew.)

He started collecting coins when he was in his early teens and kept up his interest all of his life. He especially prized his 25-year and 50-year medals for membership in the American Numismatic Association.

He always liked candy and was happy to give it to others also. When he was engaged to my mother in 1920, he had to take a trip from New York to the West Coast. In those days such a trip had to be done by train and he was gone for one month. He arranged for $500 worth of chocolate candy to be delivered to his fiancee. A portion of it was supposed to be delivered each day while he was gone. By mistake, the candy company delivered all the chocolates on one day. Remembering what one dollar would buy in 1920, it is hard to picture what a huge mound of candy must have been delivered!

When he proposed to my mother he said, "I want you to love my children too." She certainly did.

He was a gentleman in every sense of the word and most assuredly gentle. He was mild mannered and never swore, rarely raised his voice and even rarer in anger. The strongest beverage he drank was cocoa, not ever coffee or tea. He always wore a boutonniere in his buttonhole. He loved to walk, and when we lived in New Rochelle he regularly walked home from the train station. On occasion, I would go to the station to meet him. When we moved to New York he would get off the subway several stations in advance to walk to our apartment.

He was the originator of Coin Week in 1923. He and my uncle Henry (who lived next to us in New Rochelle) were partners in Guttag Brothers, which dealt in foreign exchange, securities and coins. They built their own building at 42 Stone Street in 1930 and were the first in their field to do so. My father had the solid bronze doors of the entrance to the building patterned after a New York State coin of 1785. There was a huge, time clock operated, walk-in safe in the basement of the building. A tube through which food could be sent to anyone accidentally locked into the safe was also provided. I can remember doing my best (without success) to get locked in when I was a young boy.

Guttag Brothers were very progressive and advertised over radio station WOR in about 1930 or 1931. They were the first securities and coin dealers to advertise over the radio. I still remember the punch line in the ad "Write for BTI." (This was their list of bank, trust and insurance stocks.)

For many years they had their own medallion to advertise their coin business. The medallion is basically a work of art and features a woman and a man examining a coin with the woman holding a book *NUMISMATICS* and the oil lamp symbolizing knowledge. This interest in art extended to obtaining, for our house in New Rochelle, two marble statues and an outdoor marble fountain with a sculptured water pourer, which he found on one of his trips to Italy.

Reminiscences of Julius Guttag by His Son

A trusted employee had systematically stolen gold coins from Guttag Brothers during the period between 1924 and 1928. The coin value was $39,152. The insurance company only wanted to pay the bullion value which was considerably less (for example, a $20 Utah gold piece had a coin value of $400 and a $50 gold piece had a coin value of $450).

The court upheld Guttag Brothers' contention, and they were awarded the full coin value. This was a precedent-setting case.

My father was a member of a number of numismatic organizations. These included the American Numismatic Association, the American Numismatic Society, and the New York Coin Club. He was the founder of the Westchester County Coin Club in 1934. He served as president for a number of years and retained his membership after moving to New York City and frequently went to its meetings after our move. The first few meetings of the Westchester County Coin Club were held in our living room in New Rochelle until a permanent meeting place could be found (the New Rochelle YMCA). For many years he would give coins from his business at the meetings to encourage attendance. He was a firm believer that collecting did not have to be an expensive hobby. The important thing was that it was enjoyable. Another area where he collected was silver spoons.

Joseph Lasser, as a young boy (beginning as a pre-teenager), developed an interest in coins, and my father saw to it that he was always able to attend the Westchester County Coin Club meetings.

While Pitt Skipton was primarily responsible for getting the New Rochelle commemorative half dollar, my father also was instrumental in securing the minting of the coin. My father gave each of his children one of the New Rochelle commemorative coins, and we all still have them today.

In order to keep his personal coin collection at home, he had three safes in our house. One was built into the wall of his study on the second floor, and a second one was built into the wall of the sun room when it was added to the house. The third one was a portable cabinet kept in my room. Less valuable coins were kept in it. It had a "secret" compartment, and as a boy I enjoyed pressing the hidden lever which released the compartment. One of the coins kept in the compartment was a very massive ancient Chinese coin.

Books were published based on his Latin American collection and on his collection of Civil War tokens. While his Latin American book is the more authoritative one (and has been reprinted), he spent much more time on his Civil War collection, and I can recall the time he took to point out various parts of it to me in his study. I can also recall Dr. Hetrich as a white-haired man with a long white beard, who came to our house for a week at a time to work on my father's Civil War collection. We children were told to be very quiet when he was there. Two editions were published of the Civil War collection. There was the regular one and a leatherbound limited edition of which only 15 copies were made.

My sister, Evelyn, has one copy and has advised me that the cover has disintegrated quite badly.

My father always carried a magnifying glass, (which is indispensable for a numismatist) with him. The importance of condition in coins is nothing new. He impressed its importance on me at an early age even though I never had developed a large coin collection. Instead, my interests ran to stamps, where condition is also important, but not nearly to the extent it is with coins.

Because of my interest in stamps, he took me to the International Philatelic Exhibition in New York in 1926 and obtained copies of the White Plains sheet for me. Guttag Brothers also issued a medallion for the exhibition, advertising its coin department. This was apart from their regular medallion that they used for many years to promote coin collecting. He also obtained the remnants of a worldwide stamp collection for me when I was a youngster. The highest catalogue value stamp in that collection was a Baden stamp cataloguing at $25 (it now catalogues at $1200). This led to my interest in collecting stamps of German states, and I now have a substantial stamp collection in that area.

While he lived in New Rochelle and later in New York City, he maintained his legal residence for many years at our family's summer home (originally owned by my grandfather and then jointly owned by my father and his two brothers) in Lake Pleasant, New York, in the Adirondacks. Our house was on Lake Sacandaga and was reached by a private road (about 1/2 mile) which connected to the main (dirt) road which, in turn, connected with the state highway. One time, in the 1920s, he noticed that the telephone company had placed stakes out for a telephone line along our private road. My father asked the man from the phone company why it had been done since no permission had been granted. The man from the telephone company said,

Reminiscences of Julius Guttag by His Son

"Why everyone wants a telephone." My father answered, "We don't. This is our vacation home, and if it is important enough that we must be reached, then it can be done by a telegram to the village" (about three miles away). In the 50 years the house was in our family, it never had a telephone. However, it did have electricity. We made our own electricity with the aid of a gasoline engine.

My father's interest in numismatics extended to collecting items about numismatics. Thus, when editorial cartoons or comic strips depicted numismatic subject matter, he would get signed originals from the artists. One that I can remember was a Toonerville Trolley one-panel comic strip signed by Fontaine Fox, the artist and author of the strip. The "blurb" states that numismatists who have heard of the conductor's coin collection are always disappointed when they see it because all the coins are counterfeits.

He had an extremely good memory, especially for history, and he retained this even after he had sleeping sickness in his early 40s, which illness later led to Parkinsonism, the cause of his death. He was also very good at mathematics and had an uncanny ability to detect forged paper money and counterfeit coins.

One time, in his business, he was offered a certified check of $1,000. He was suspicious about it and phoned the bank that had issued the check. The bank verified the fact that it had issued the check and it was good. Nevertheless, my father refused to accept the check. About 10 minutes after he had turned down the man who had offered it to him, the bank phoned, quite excitedly, that yes, they had certified it as a $10 check but it had been raised to $1,000.

I worked for him one summer during my vacation. A man who was going to England wanted a 1,000 pound note. At the time the pound was worth just a little under $5. The 1,000 pound note was the largest piece of single currency I have ever held in my hands. The man paid for it with $5,000 in cash and a $40 check which bounced!

He never lost his interest in numismatics, even in his old age, long after he had disposed of his most valuable collections. Instead he found other areas of numismatic interest.

The North West Company Token

by *Thomas S. LaMarre* RCR 69 1988

Scrawled in a mixture of vermilion and grease on a rock in the channel was the inscription "Alexander Mackenzie, from Canada, by land, the twenty-second of July, one thousand seven hundred and ninety-three."

Mackenzie, an agent of the North West Company, reached the Pacific through North America 12 years before Lewis and Clark. Over a century later, commemorative gold dollars dated 1904 and 1905 and the Series 1901 $10 Legal Tender note honored Lewis and Clark. The North West Company's link with numismatics is more obscure, and is in the form of the brass token pictured in the *Guide Book of United States Coins*. It was struck in 1820, the year Mackenzie died.

The Montreal-based North West Company, one of the giants of the fur trade, was a bitter and powerful rival of the Hudson's Bay Company. The name was first used in the 1770s by Montreal traders, primarily Scottish immigrants, who pooled their resources to reduce competition. Three years later a new temporary organization took the name. It issued 16 shares of stock held by nine partnerships. One of the partners was Simon McTavish, who lived in Montreal like a lord and dominated the North West Company for many years. McTavish helped form a more permanent North West Company in the winter of 1783-84. It had offices in Beaver Hall, overlooking the river, and a select group of employees soon formed a dining group called The Beaver Club. Members were required to have spent at least one winter in Indian country. They wore large gold club medals when they met.

"1793. May 10. Signed my engagement with the North West Company for five years to winter in the Indian country as a clerk," John Macdonnel wrote in his diary. "The terms are 100 pounds at the expiration, and found in necessaries."

The rugged voyageurs of the North West Company penetrated deep into the continent, paddling and portaging their trade goods under conditions that would break ordinary men.

"They are short, thick-set, and active, and never tire," a contemporary description of the voyageurs said. "A Canadian, if born to be a laborer, deems himself to be very unfortunate if he should chance to grow over five feet five or six inches. And if he shall reach five feet ten or eleven, it forever excludes him from the privilege of becoming a voyageur. There is no room for the legs of such people in these canoes.

"But if he shall stop growing at about five feet four inches, and be gifted with a good voice and lungs that never tire, he is considered as having been born under a most favorable star."

Brigades of birch-bark canoes, loaded with trade goods and led by experienced guides, left Montreal in late May. A writer who traveled in one of the parties reported, "These canoes were exceedingly strong and capacious, they were about 36 feet in length by six feet wide near the middle; and although the birch bark which formed a thin external coating for their ribs of white cedar, and their longitudinal laths of the same wood appeared to compose but a flimsy vessel, yet they usually carried a weight of five tons."

It took the voyageurs six weeks to reach Grand Portage, on the far side of Lake Superior. There they exchanged their cargoes for pelts brought by the "North Men." The two groups had to return to their respective bases by October or face starvation in the wilderness during the winter.

By 1795 the North West Company controlled more than two-thirds of the lucrative Canadian fur trade. According to Don Taxay's *Money of the American Indians and Other Primitive Currencies of the Americas* (Nummus Press, 1970), the trading activities of the company's agents made Indians aware of the immediate negotiability of furs, particularly beaver skins. An early 18th-century registry of goods sold to the Indians listed such items as yard broadcloth, three beaver skins; six knives, one beaver skin; one hat, two beaver skins; one shirt, one beaver skin; and two small axes, one beaver skin.

The North West Company Token

The equation of beaver skins with wealth is evident in an entry in agent David Thompson's journal: "We came to an aged Indian, his arms folded across his breast with a pensive countenance, looking at the beavers swimming in the water and carrying their winter provisions to their houses... 'We are now killing the beaver without labor; we are now rich, but shall soon be poor, for when the beaver are destroyed we have nothing to depend on to purchase what we want for our families; strangers now overrun our country with their iron traps and we and they shall soon be poor.'"

The monetary use of beavers became so well established that the Hudson's Bay Company issued copper beaver-shaped tokens that circulated at the value of one skin apiece.

The copper and brass North West Company tokens were struck in 1820, probably by John Walker & Co. of Birmingham, England, or Cotterill, Hill & Co. of nearby Walsall. Alfred Sandham's *Coins, Tokens and Medals of the Dominion of Canada,* published in 1869, identified the obverse bust as George IV. In an article in the November 1961 issue of the *Canadian Journal of Numismatics,* author R.C. Willey identified it as George III. Most collectors simply refer to the portrait as a laureate bust.

On the reverse was a beaver on a log, foreshadowing the design of today's Canadian five-cent piece.

Breton's 1894 catalogue had a drawing of the North West Company token and noted, "It is now very rare, not over five or six specimens being known of which four are to be found in the collections of: Mr. Thomas Wilson of Clarence, Ontario; Rev. Father Milchaud, C.S.V., of Montreal; Mr. W. Bastian, also of Montreal, and the last one in the Ottawa government's collection."

In 1902 J.C. Trenaman wrote, "This piece is now the rarest of brass coins," but this assessment proved to be misleading. In "Notes on the North West Company Token" (April 1971, *TAMS Journal),* author Donald M. Stewart estimated that 5,000 tokens were minted, of which approximately 200 are known to exist.

All but one known specimen are holed; the unholed specimen was auctioned at the 1952 ANA Convention and was acquired by Douglas Ferguson of Canada. It was described as being in Very Good condition. All of the tokens have been found in Indian burial grounds in the region of the lower Columbia River and Umpqua River valleys in Oregon, where the pieces were among other artifacts.

Donald Stewart speculated that the tokens were probably used as counters at the fort. They were holed for distribution to the Indians. The holes are of uniform size and position.

Other numismatists believe that the North West Company tokens were paid to the Indians for furs and could be used to make purchases. A token was presumably valued at "One Made Beaver."

The tokens were holed so that they could be suspended on cords or wires, for the Indians did not have purses or pocketbooks. One museum has a collection of 14 North West Company tokens strung on a strip of rawhide. Most known specimens exhibit wear resulting from suspension and corrosion from being buried.

The North West Company went out of existence one year after the tokens were struck. During the boom years of the fur trade, the company's voyageurs had brought out 20,000 beaver annually, most of which were auctioned in England or exported to Europe and Asia. However, the rivalry with the Hudson's Bay Company turned into an all-out war that proved fatal to the North West Company in 1811-12. Lord Selkirk bought a controlling interest in the Hudson's Bay Company. His goal was to establish an agricultural colony in the plains of the Red River area, south of Lake Winnipeg, in what is now Manitoba.

The North West Company tried to block the plan by buying Hudson's Bay Company stock in London and by discouraging potential colonists, but both efforts failed.

The settlers were poor farmers. Facing starvation, they seized provisions from the North West Company's posts. Fighting broke out at many locations, and 23 people died in a battle on the Red River. The feud ended in 1821 when the two companies merged and the Hudson's Bay Company took over the North West Company's posts. At the time of the merger, the Hudson's Bay Company had 76 posts, while the North West Company had 97.

In 1854 the Hudson's Bay Company struck a set of tokens for its Eastmain District, a region which now includes parts of northern Ontario and west central Quebec. There were four denominations of tokens: one-eighth made beaver, one-fourth made beaver, one-half made beaver, and one made beaver. The pieces were erroneously inscribed NB for new beaver instead of MB for made beaver, which was the generally accepted standard of exchange. On the obverse of the tokens was the crest of the Hudson's Bay Company within an oak

The North West Company Token

wreath composed of two branches tied together below. The joined letters HB appeared on the reverse with the denomination.

The November 1945 issue of *The Numismatist* reported: "A recent addition to our collection of doubtful classifications is a curious uniface copper piece bearing the inscription 2 F.S.B. 1858. It was attributed by an English dealer to the Canadian Northwest. Classifying it as an 'unpublished token' he extended the abbreviation to read F(UR) B(EAVER) S(KINS). While this may seem far-fetched, his attribution should not be dismissed until a better one is found... If it were not for the pedigree of this piece (it was once part of a splendid collection of British colonials) we would refuse to make our speculations public."

The Hudson's Bay Company exists today as the largest retailer in Canada, operating nearly 600 stores, and it remains one of the largest fur-trading companies in the world.

The 1804 and 1823 "Restrike" Cents

by Q. David Bowers — 1993

The following was written for "The Joys of Collecting" column in COIN WORLD, 1993.

Among the most curious coins in the 19th-century series of large cents are the so-called "restrikes" dated 1804 and 1823. You will find them listed and priced in the *Guide Book,* and also offered in auction and sale offerings. Today, these are recognized for what they are: concoctions, of a sort, made outside of the Mint, by combining irrelevant dies in order to create "1804" and "1823" cents for collectors. In my opinion, the intent was more to make curiosities, than to deceive. The fabrications are very obvious.

Recently, when looking through old catalogues, I came across one issued by Lancaster, Pennsylvania dealer Charles Steigerwalt in January 1907. The following essay, new to my eyes, was included:

"SO-CALLED MINT RESTRIKE CENTS: A certain kind of 1804 and 1823 cents have appeared in sale catalogues for years as 'Mint Restrikes.' The recent cataloguers may be excused on the plea of ignorance, but when these rank counterfeits are sold by those who have being doing so for years, it is time collectors knew their true character.

"While at a recent sale, lacking information regarding the 1823 was given by an aged collector, who told how, years ago, he had found the dies in New York, probably sold with old iron from the mint, brought them to Philadelphia, had a collar made, which was lacking, and the coins struck by a man named Miller on 7th Street in that city.

"Later, the dies came into possession of a then leading dealer there and, when his store was sold out in 1885, the writer finding them among a lot of old dies purchased, they were at once destroyed so effectually that no more will ever come from that source. These coins never saw the Mint, and are counterfeits pure and simple.

"It was supposed the 1804 came from the same source as the 1823, but the originator of those disclaimed any knowledge of the 1804. An effort was made in a recent sale catalogue to throw an air of mystery around this 1804. That is simply ridiculous. The obverse has been identified as an 1803, but as that date was too common, a crude 4 was cut over the 3 and a reverse of the same period after the fraction was omitted, probably of about 1816 or later, was used in striking these abominations. By whom struck is unknown, but it was at a period long after, when the dies were rusty, and certainly not in the Mint."

Machin's Mills Bicentennial

by Gary A. Trudgen   RCR 64 1987

The year 1987 marks the passage of two centuries since one of the most interesting state coinage operations was organized. On April 18, 1787, Thomas Machin, along with five copartners, legally bound themselves together with the intent to coin money. One month earlier, on March 3rd, Machin filed a petition with the New York State Legislature requesting a grant to coin copper for the state.

Machin had excellent connections within the New York Assembly committee that was assigned to investigate the establishment of a copper coinage in the state. Thus, he was probably confident that he would be granted his request. One of his copartners, David Brooks, was a member of this three-man committee. Alexander Hamilton, who became one of our great American statesmen, was another member of the committee. The third member was John Lansing, who had strong political ties with Governor George Clinton. Thomas Machin and George Clinton were good friends. Governor Clinton was an opponent of the Constitution and would have favored any legislation which could have given more power to the state, such as their own coinage. Thus, Brooks and Lansing should have favored a state coinage, however, Hamilton would have opposed it because he was a zealous Federalist. Somehow, Hamilton's views won out, and Thomas Machin did not receive a coinage grant. As a result, Machin's newly formed coinage firm quickly allied themselves with another coinage firm. On June 7, 1787 they merged with Reuben Harmon's Rupert, Vermont firm, which held a coinage grant from the Republic of Vermont.

Fortunately, the Machin's Mills indenture has survived the ages and is now in the custody of the American Numismatic Society. It consists of two leaves of good rag paper on which there are three pages of handwritten text. Following the text are the signatures of the proprietors along with red wax seals, cracked with age. The indenture measures 47.5 cm. x 34 cm. (18.7 x 13.4 inches) and is bound.

Within the text of this historic document are the articles of agreement between the six copartners: Samuel Atlee, James F. Atlee, David Brooks, James Giles, James Grier, and Thomas Machin. We find they agreed to establish their company for a period of seven years, each of them contributing 50 pounds of current New York money toward a joint capital of 300 pounds. Thomas Machin would allow the use of his mills free of charge for conducting their business. Samuel Atlee and James Atlee would lend, free of charge, certain implements that were required for the business. These "certain implements" were undoubtedly the coining machinery required to convert Thomas Machin's mills into a mint.[1] The other three copartners were to contribute 10 pounds each of New York money toward completing the works for carrying on their business. James Giles was to be the cashier and bookkeeper, while James Atlee and Thomas Machin were to equally manage the minting of coins. All other aspects of the business were to be handled jointly by Samuel Atlee, David Brooks, and James Grier.

The Machin's Mills coinage operation took place on land owned by Governor George Clinton. This land, consisting of 108 acres, was located along the eastern shore of Great Pond, now Orange Lake, a few miles west of Newburgh, New York. It was part of a large tract of land known as the Baird Land Patent that had been granted on February 28, 1716.[2] George Clinton had purchased the land from Munson Ward on March 20, 1782. After the Revolutionary War ended in April 1783, he allowed Thomas Machin to settle on it. Machin cut timber from the area, built a dwelling, and named the area New Grange. He and his wife, Susan, moved into their new home near the end of May 1783. In 1784 Machin opened a new outlet for Great Pond by digging a canal at the point where water overflowed during times of high water The water provided by the canal flowed into Chambers Creek, now known as Quassaic Creek. He then built a grist and saw mill at the end of the canal just before it branched into Chambers Creek. The building spanned the canal lengthwise with a paddle waterwheel mounted within the canal directly beneath the structure. It was this building that was converted into a coinage mint in 1787 by Thomas Machin and his associates. The mint was constructed from wood, and measured 30 feet wide and 40 feet long, and was two stories high. After the mint closed, Machin converted the building back to a grist mill before he moved from the area in January 1791. On October 29, 1793, George Clinton sold the property to David Byrns and Hugh Walsh.

An excellent description of the operation of the mint has come down to us from Machin's son, Thomas N. Machin, Jr.:[3]

"The metal used was copper, obtained by melting up cannon and leaving out the zinc in the alloy. The copper was then run into moulds, and rolled into flat sheets the thickness of the coin and from one to two feet wide. It was then punched with a screw, moved by a lever, so adjusted that half a revolution would press out a disk the size of the coin. The blanks were then put into a cylinder and revolved with sand, saw-dust, and water. They were generally left revolving through the night; and the coiners circulated the story that the devil came by night to work for them. They also sometimes worked in masks to create a terror in the neighborhood. In one night the cylinder would wear the edges of the blanks smooth. The coining press was a screw, with an iron bar about 10 feet long through the top. On each end of this bar was a leaden weight of perhaps 500 pounds. The threads of the screw were large and square and worked through an iron frame. Ropes were attached to each end of the bar, and it was swung about halfway around by two men pulling upon the ropes; two other men pulled the lever back, and a fifth laid on the blank with his fingers. The last operative named sat in a pit so that the lever would not touch his head. The coinage was about 60 per minute. A little silver was coined, but mostly copper, and the work was continued four or five years. Atlee, the engraver, wore a horrid mask, and frightened some boys who came to fish so they never ventured near the mill again."

The preceding description by Machin's son of the operation of the mint not only gives good technical details of early American coinage technology but also gives some insight into how the mint interacted with the surrounding community. Obviously the coiners wanted to keep the public away. They used scare tactics, such as wearing horrid masks as they worked and circulating stories that the devil came at night to work for them. We can only speculate as to why they did this, of which there are a couple of possibilities. First, they probably felt a need for secrecy because they made some silver coins[4] and several types of copper coins without proper authorization. The private mintage of silver coin which held legal tender status was a serious legal violation and was punishable by death. Their unauthorized coinage of copper was not that serious and was normally overlooked by the authorities because copper coin was not legal tender in the 18th century. Second, because of the nature of their business, the coiners may have wanted to keep the public away for security.

The copper coins produced by Machin's private mint are some of the most interesting from the state coinage era. They made their lightweight versions of other coppers, that were then circulating in our country, in the interest of making a profit. Numismatic study has shown that they initially made imitation British halfpennies. They then produced several different Connecticut and Vermont coppers. Finally, in 1789, near the end of their operation during the copper crisis, they made some interesting mules (irrelevant die combinations), and a few New Jersey copper varieties struck over other coppers of their day. In short, Machin's Mills has provided the numismatist with a bonanza of intriguing coins from our country's early days to study and collect.

Today, the Machin's Mills site rests quietly in a relatively undisturbed wooded area by the lake. Machin's canal and the northeast corner of the mint foundation can still be seen. Machin's home, just south of the mint, was standing in 1955 when Eric Newman and Wayte Raymond visited the area. Unfortunately, only the foundation of his home remains today. On Saturday, September 24, 1984, a historical marker, placed near the site of the mint, was dedicated in commemoration of Machin's Mills.[5]

Thanks to Machin's Mills, our numismatic heritage is all the richer. Consider learning more about their coinage operation and the coins they produced. Perhaps you will become enthralled, as I have, with this fascinating early American coinage episode.

Acknowledgments

Special thanks are due Francis D. Campbell, ANS librarian, for 'his help in connection with the Machin's Mills indenture.

Notes

1 This coinage machinery was probably the same that had been used the previous year (1786) in New York City to strike coppers from dies engraved by James Atlee. These coppers are several varieties of

imitation British halfpennies, a few bust right Connecticut varieties, and the Non Vi Virtute Vici pattern.

2 The Baird Patent, which consisted of 6,000 acres, was issued to Alexander Baird, Abraham Van Vlecque, and Hermanus Johnson. During the 18th century it was part of Ulster County, however, on April 3, 1801, it became part of Orange County when the latter county was expanded.

3 E.M. Ruttenber, in his *History of the County of Orange: With a History of the Town and City of Newburgh, 1875,* published this description of the coinage operation by Machin's son, which was obtained from Dr. F.B. Hough of Albany, New York.

4 The limited silver coinage that Machin's Mills produced may be an unlisted variety of Massachusetts Pine Tree shilling that is found struck over 1781 Mexican one-real pieces of Charles 111. Issue No. 69 of *The Colonial Newsletter* contains an article by the author on this subject.

5 The historical marker was proposed by the author and Oliver Shipp, the town of Newburgh historian. It was funded by the Newburgh Coin Club, the Orange County government, and the author. Colin Faulds, the Orange County historian, coordinated the effort, and the town of Newburgh installed the marker.

Call To Arms— Collectors Unite!

| by Q. David Bowers | 1993 |

The following was written for "The Joys of Collecting" column in COIN WORLD, 1993.

If you are interested in commemoratives, you know that a half century or so ago, in the 1930s, commemoratives were front row, center as the most talked-about topic in numismatics. Back then, collectors either loved commemoratives or they hated them. Those who disliked the new coins—and the year 1936, the height of the boom—saw nearly 20 new designs of half dollars being marketed—felt that numismatists were being exploited. Collectors were being made to pay for various statues, celebrations, and other events via premiums charged for coins by various local and private issuing "commissions." It can be argued that collectors were not forced to buy the new coins. However, every numismatist desired to have completion in his or her collection. If a new issue existed, it could not be ignored.

Now we are in 1993. The same things are happening, except that the culprit is the United States Congress. Private commissions are no more, but have been replaced by an insidious new feature, the "surcharge," whereby purchasers of coins are forced (as part of a coin's purchase price) to donate to the restoration of Civil War battlefields, upkeep of the White House, or even the general fund of the U.S. Treasury. Moreover, as the IRS has ruled that such donations are not tax deductible, collectors lose both ways. And as if this were not bad enough, the issue prices—even before the surcharges are added—are so high that there is only a remote chance that the purchaser of a new commemorative coin or set can make a profit in the next several years if the coins are sold.

By one calculation, the 27—count them, 27—different Uncirculated and Proof versions of coins planned for the 1996 Olympics will cost collectors about $2,500 for the group! This completely wipes out the chance that youngsters and beginning collectors can enjoy the ownership of such a set. A greater turn-off to numismatics cannot be imagined! It is Congress, not the U.S. Mint, that is responsible for such programs. OUR CONGRESS is doing this TO US. As the numismatic community has no control over the surcharges, no control over the asking prices, no control over the mintages, and no control over the designs, it is 1776 revisited: Taxation without representation. Perhaps it is time for a numismatic "Revolutionary War."